Nutshell Series

of

WEST PUBLISHING COMPANY

P.O. Box 3526

St. Paul, Minnesota 55165

February, 1982

———

I

Community Property, 1982, approx. 350 pages, by Robert L. Mennell, Professor of Law, Hamline University.

Comparative Legal Traditions, 1982, approx. 385 pages, by Mary Ann Glendon, Professor of Law, Boston College, Michael Wallace Gordon, Professor of Law, University of Florida and Christopher Osakwe, Professor of Law, Tulane University.

Conflicts, 1982, approx. 469 pages, by David D. Siegel, Professor of Law, Albany Law School, Union University.

Constitutional Analysis, 1979, 388 pages, by Jerre S. Williams, former Professor of Law, University of Texas.

Constitutional Power—Federal and State, 1974, 411 pages, by David E. Engdahl, former Professor of Law, University of Denver.

Consumer Law, 2nd Ed., 1981, 418 pages, by David G. Epstein, Dean and Professor of Law, University of Arkansas and Steve H. Nickles, Professor of Law, University of Arkansas.

Contracts, 1975, 307 pages, by Gordon D. Schaber, Dean and Professor of Law, McGeorge School of Law and Claude D. Rohwer, Professor of Law, McGeorge School of Law.

Contract Remedies, 1981, 323 pages, by Jane M. Friedman, Professor of Law, Wayne State University.

Corporations—Law of, 1980, 379 pages, by Robert W. Hamilton, Professor of Law, University of Texas.

Corrections and Prisoners' Rights—Law of, 1976, 353 pages, by Sheldon Krantz, Dean and Professor of Law, University of San Diego.

Criminal Law, 1975, 302 pages, by Arnold H. Loewy, Professor of Law, University of North Carolina.

Criminal Procedure—Constitutional Limitations, 3rd Ed., 1980, 438 pages, by Jerold H. Israel, Professor of Law,

University of Michigan and Wayne R. LaFave, Professor of Law, University of Illinois.

Debtor-Creditor Law, 2nd Ed., 1980, 324 pages, by David G. Epstein, Dean and Professor of Law, University of Arkansas.

Employment Discrimination—Federal Law of, 2nd Ed., 1981, 402 pages, by Mack A. Player, Professor of Law, University of Georgia.

Energy Law, 1981, 338 pages, by Joseph P. Tomain, Professor of Law, Drake University.

Estate Planning—Introduction to, 2nd Ed., 1978, 378 pages, by Robert J. Lynn, Professor of Law, Ohio State University.

Evidence, Federal Rules of, 1981, 428 pages, by Michael H. Graham, Professor of Law, University of Illinois.

Evidence, State and Federal Rules, 2nd Ed., 1981, 514 pages, by Paul F. Rothstein, Professor of Law, Georgetown University.

Family Law, 1977, 400 pages, by Harry D. Krause, Professor of Law, University of Illinois.

Federal Estate and Gift Taxation, 2nd Ed., 1979, 488 pages, by John K. McNulty, Professor of Law, University of California, Berkeley.

Federal Income Taxation of Individuals, 2nd Ed., 1978, 422 pages, by John K. McNulty, Professor of Law, University of California, Berkeley.

Federal Income Taxation of Corporations and Stockholders, 2nd Ed., 1981, 362 pages, by Jonathan Sobeloff, Late Professor of Law, Georgetown University and Peter P. Weidenbruch, Jr., Professor of Law, Georgetown University.

Federal Jurisdiction, 2nd Ed., 1981, 258 pages, by David P. Currie, Professor of Law, University of Chicago.

Future Interests, 1981, 361 pages, by Lawrence W. Waggoner, Professor of Law, University of Michigan.

Government Contracts, 1979, 423 pages, by W. Noel Keyes, Professor of Law, Pepperdine University.

Historical Introduction to Anglo-American Law, 2nd Ed., 1973, 280 pages, by Frederick G. Kempin, Jr., Professor of Business Law, Wharton School of Finance and Commerce, University of Pennsylvania.

Injunctions, 1974, 264 pages, by John F. Dobbyn, Professor of Law, Villanova University.

Insurance Law, 1981, 281 pages, by John F. Dobbyn, Professor of Law, Villanova University.

International Business Transactions, 1981, 393 pages, by Donald T. Wilson, Professor of Law, Loyola University, Los Angeles.

Judicial Process, 1980, 292 pages, by William L. Reynolds, Professor of Law, University of Maryland.

Jurisdiction, 4th Ed., 1980, 232 pages, by Albert A. Ehrenzweig, Late Professor of Law, University of California, Berkeley, David W. Louisell, Late Professor of Law, University of California, Berkeley and Geoffrey C. Hazard, Jr., Professor of Law, Yale Law School.

Juvenile Courts, 2nd Ed., 1977, 275 pages, by Sanford J. Fox, Professor of Law, Boston College.

Labor Arbitration Law and Practice, 1979, 358 pages, by Dennis R. Nolan, Professor of Law, University of South Carolina.

Labor Law, 1979, 403 pages, by Douglas L. Leslie, Professor of Law, University of Virginia.

Land Use, 1978, 316 pages, by Robert R. Wright, Professor of Law, University of Arkansas, Little Rock and Susan Webber, Professor of Law, University of Arkansas, Little Rock.

Landlord and Tenant Law, 1979, 319 pages, by David S. Hill, Professor of Law, University of Colorado.

Law Study and Law Examinations—Introduction to, 1971, 389 pages, by Stanley V. Kinyon, Late Professor of Law, University of Minnesota.

Legal Interviewing and Counseling, 1976, 353 pages, by Thomas L. Shaffer, Professor of Law, Washington and Lee University.

Legal Research, 3rd Ed., 1978, 415 pages, by Morris L. Cohen, Professor of Law and Law Librarian, Yale University.

Legal Writing, 1982, approx. 250 pages, by Dr. Lynn B. Squires, University of Washington School of Law and Marjorie Dick Rombauer, Professor of Law, University of Washington.

Legislative Law and Process, 1975, 279 pages, by Jack Davies, Professor of Law, William Mitchell College of Law.

Local Government Law, 1975, 386 pages, by David J. McCarthy, Jr., Dean and Professor of Law, Georgetown University.

Mass Communications Law, 1977, 431 pages, by Harvey L. Zuckman, Professor of Law, Catholic University and Martin J. Gaynes, Lecturer in Law, Temple University.

Medical Malpractice—The Law of, 1977, 340 pages, by Joseph H. King, Professor of Law, University of Tennessee.

Military Law, 1980, 378 pages, by Charles A. Shanor, Professor of Law, Emory University and Timothy P. Terrell, Professor of Law, Emory University.

Post-Conviction Remedies, 1978, 360 pages, by Robert Popper, Professor of Law, University of Missouri, Kansas City.

Presidential Power, 1977, 328 pages, by Arthur Selwyn Miller, Professor of Law Emeritus, George Washington University.

Procedure Before Trial, 1972, 258 pages, by Delmar Karlen, Professor of Law, College of William and Mary.

Products Liability, 2nd Ed., 1981, 341 pages, by Dix W. Noel, Late Professor of Law, University of Tennessee and Jerry J. Phillips, Professor of Law, University of Tennessee.

Professional Responsibility, 1980, 399 pages, by Robert H. Aronson, Professor of Law, University of Washington, and Donald T. Weckstein, Professor of Law, University of San Diego.

Real Estate Finance, 1979, 292 pages, by Jon W. Bruce, Professor of Law, Vanderbilt University.

Real Property, 2nd Ed., 1981, 448 pages, by Roger H. Bernhardt, Professor of Law, Golden Gate University.

Regulated Industries, 1982, approx. 394 pages, by Ernest Gellhorn, Professor of Law, University of Virginia, and Richard J. Pierce, Professor of Law, Tulane University.

Remedies, 1977, 364 pages, by John F. O'Connell, Professor of Law, Western State University College of Law, Fullerton.

Res Judicata, 1976, 310 pages, by Robert C. Casad, Professor of Law, University of Kansas.

Sales, 2nd Ed., 1981, 370 pages, by John M. Stockton, Professor of Business Law, Wharton School of Finance and Commerce, University of Pennsylvania.

Secured Transactions, 2nd Ed., 1981, 391 pages, by Henry J. Bailey, Professor of Law, Willamette University.

Securities Regulation, 1978, 300 pages, by David L. Ratner, Professor of Law, Cornell University.

Sex Discrimination, 1982, approx. 386 pages, by Claire Sherman Thomas, lecturer, University of Washington, Women's Studies Department.

Titles—The Calculus of Interests, 1968, 277 pages, by Oval A. Phipps, Late Professor of Law, St. Louis University.

Torts—Injuries to Persons and Property, 1977, 434 pages, by Edward J. Kionka, Professor of Law, Southern Illinois University.

Torts—Injuries to Family, Social and Trade Relations, 1979, 358 pages, by Wex S. Malone, Professor of Law Emeritus, Louisiana State University.

Trial Advocacy, 1979, 402 pages, by Paul B. Bergman, Adjunct Professor of Law, University of California, Los Angeles.

Trial and Practice Skills, 1978, 346 pages, by Kenney F. Hegland, Professor of Law, University of Arizona.

Trial, The First—Where Do I Sit? What Do I Say?, 1982, approx. 399 pages, by Steven H. Goldberg, Professor of Law, University of Arkansas, Little Rock.

Uniform Commercial Code, 1975, 507 pages, by Bradford Stone, Professor of Law, Detroit College of Law.

Uniform Probate Code, 1978, 425 pages, by Lawrence H. Averill, Jr., Professor of Law, University of Wyoming.

Welfare Law—Structure and Entitlement, 1979, 455 pages, by Arthur B. LaFrance, Professor of Law, University of Maine.

Wills and Trusts, 1979, 392 pages, by Robert L. Mennell, Professor of Law, Hamline University.

Hornbook Series

and

Basic Legal Texts

of

WEST PUBLISHING COMPANY

P.O. Box 3526

St. Paul, Minnesota 55165

February, 1982

———

Administrative Law, Davis' Text on, 3rd Ed., 1972, 617 pages, by Kenneth Culp Davis, Professor of Law, University of San Diego.

Agency, Seavey's Hornbook on, 1964, 329 pages, by Warren A. Seavey, Late Professor of Law, Harvard University.

Agency and Partnership, Reuschlein & Gregory's Hornbook on the Law of, 1979 with 1981 Pocket Part, 625 pages, by Harold Gill Reuschlein, Professor of Law, St. Mary's University and William A. Gregory, Professor of Law, Southern Illinois University.

Antitrust, Sullivan's Hornbook on the Law of, 1977, 886 pages, by Lawrence A. Sullivan, Professor of Law, University of California, Berkeley.

Common Law Pleading, Koffler and Reppy's Hornbook on, 1969, 663 pages, by Joseph H. Koffler, Professor of Law, New York Law School and Alison Reppy, Late Dean and Professor of Law, New York Law School.

Common Law Pleading, Shipman's Hornbook on, 3rd Ed., 1923, 644 pages, by Henry W. Ballentine, Late Professor of Law, University of California, Berkeley.

Conflict of Laws, Scoles and Hay's Hornbook on, 1982, approx. 950 pages, by Eugene F. Scoles, Professor of Law, University of Oregon and Peter Hay, Dean and Professor of Law, University of Illinois.

Constitutional Law, Nowak, Rotunda and Young's Hornbook on, 1978 with 1982 Pocket Part, 974 pages, by John E. Nowak, Professor of Law, University of Illinois, Ronald D. Rotunda, Professor of Law, University of Illinois, and J. Nelson Young, Professor of Law, University of North Carolina.

Contracts, Calamari and Perillo's Hornbook on, 2nd Ed., 1977, 878 pages, by John D. Calamari, Professor of Law, Fordham University and Joseph M. Perillo, Professor of Law, Fordham University.

Contracts, Corbin's One Volume Student Ed., 1952, 1224 pages, by Arthur L. Corbin, Late Professor of Law, Yale University.

Contracts, Simpson's Hornbook on, 2nd Ed., 1965, 510 pages, by Laurence P. Simpson, Late Professor of Law, New York University.

Corporate Taxation, Kahn's Handbook on, 3rd Ed., Student Ed., Soft cover, 1981, 614 pages, by Douglas A. Kahn, Professor of Law, University of Michigan.

Corporations, Henn's Hornbook on, 2nd Ed., 1970, 956 pages, by Harry G. Henn, Professor of Law, Cornell University.

Criminal Law, LaFave and Scott's Hornbook on, 1972, 763 pages, by Wayne R. LaFave, Professor of Law, University of Illinois, and Austin Scott, Jr., Late Professor of Law, University of Colorado.

Damages, McCormick's Hornbook on, 1935, 811 pages, by Charles T. McCormick, Late Dean and Professor of Law, University of Texas.

HORNBOOKS & BASIC TEXTS

Domestic Relations, Clark's Hornbook on, 1968, 754 pages, by Homer H. Clark, Jr., Professor of Law, University of Colorado.

Environmental Law, Rodgers' Hornbook on, 1977, 956 pages, by William H. Rodgers, Jr., Professor of Law, University of Washington.

Equity, McClintock's Hornbook on, 2nd Ed., 1948, 643 pages, by Henry L. McClintock, Late Professor of Law, University of Minnesota.

Estate and Gift Taxes, Lowndes, Kramer and McCord's Hornbook on, 3rd Ed., 1974, 1099 pages, by Charles L. B. Lowndes, Late Professor of Law, Duke University, Robert Kramer, Professor of Law Emeritus, George Washington University, and John H. McCord, Professor of Law, University of Illinois.

Evidence, Lilly's Introduction to, 1978, 486 pages, by Graham C. Lilly, Professor of Law, University of Virginia.

Evidence, McCormick's Hornbook on, 2nd Ed., 1972 with 1978 Pocket Part, 938 pages, General Editor, Edward W. Cleary, Professor of Law Emeritus, Arizona State University.

Federal Courts, Wright's Hornbook on, 3rd Ed., 1976, 818 pages, including Federal Rules Appendix, by Charles Alan Wright, Professor of Law, University of Texas.

Future Interest, Simes' Hornbook on, 2nd Ed., 1966, 355 pages, by Lewis M. Simes, Late Professor of Law, University of Michigan.

Income Taxation, Chommie's Hornbook on, 2nd Ed., 1973, 1051 pages, by John C. Chommie, Late Professor of Law, University of Miami.

Insurance, Keeton's Basic Text on, 1971, 712 pages, by Robert E. Keeton, Professor of Law Emeritus, Harvard University.

HORNBOOKS & BASIC TEXTS

Labor Law, Gorman's Basic Text on, 1976, 914 pages, by Robert A. Gorman, Professor of Law, University of Pennsylvania.

Law Problems, Ballentine's, 5th Ed., 1975, 767 pages, General Editor, William E. Burby, Professor of Law Emeritus, University of Southern California.

Legal Writing Style, Weihofen's, 2nd Ed., 1980, 332 pages, by Henry Weihofen, Professor of Law Emeritus, University of New Mexico.

Local Government Law, Reynolds' Hornbook on, 1982, approx. 780 pages, by Osborne M. Reynolds, Professor of Law, University of Oklahoma.

New York Practice, Siegel's Hornbook on, 1978, with 1979–80 Pocket Part, 1011 pages, by David D. Siegel, Professor of Law, Albany Law School of Union University.

Oil and Gas, Hemingway's Hornbook on, 1971 with 1979 Pocket Part, 486 pages, by Richard W. Hemingway, Professor of Law, University of Oklahoma.

Partnership, Crane and Bromberg's Hornbook on, 1968, 695 pages, by Alan R. Bromberg, Professor of Law, Southern Methodist University.

Poor, Law of the, LaFrance, Schroeder, Bennett and Boyd's Hornbook on, 1973, 558 pages, by Arthur B. LaFrance, Professor of Law, University of Maine, Milton R. Schroeder, Professor of Law, Arizona State University, Robert W. Bennett, Professor of Law, Northwestern University and William E. Boyd, Professor of Law, University of Arizona.

Property, Boyer's Survey of, 3rd Ed., 1981, 766 pages, by Ralph E. Boyer, Professor of Law, University of Miami.

Real Estate Finance Law, Osborne, Nelson and Whitman's Hornbook on, (successor to Hornbook on Mortgages), 1979, 885 pages, by George E. Osborne, Late

Professor of Law, Stanford University, Grant S. Nelson, Professor of Law, University of Missouri, Columbia and Dale A. Whitman, Professor of Law, University of Washington.

Real Property, Burby's Hornbook on, 3rd Ed., 1965, 490 pages, by William E. Burby, Professor of Law Emeritus, University of Southern California.

Real Property, Moynihan's Introduction to, 1962, 254 pages, by Cornelius J. Moynihan, Professor of Law, Suffolk University.

Remedies, Dobb's Hornbook on, 1973, 1067 pages, by Dan B. Dobbs, Professor of Law, University of Arizona.

Sales, Nordstrom's Hornbook on, 1970, 600 pages, by Robert J. Nordstrom, former Professor of Law, Ohio State University.

Secured Transactions under the U.C.C., Henson's Hornbook on, 2nd Ed., 1979, with 1979 Pocket Part, 504 pages, by Ray D. Henson, Professor of Law, University of California, Hastings College of the Law.

Torts, Prosser's Hornbook on, 4th Ed., 1971, 1208 pages, by William L. Prosser, Late Dean and Professor of Law, University of California, Berkeley.

Trial Advocacy, Jeans' Handbook on, Student Ed., Soft cover, 1975, by James W. Jeans, Professor of Law, University of Missouri, Kansas City.

Trusts, Bogert's Hornbook on, 5th Ed., 1973, 726 pages, by George G. Bogert, Late Professor of Law, University of Chicago and George T. Bogert, Attorney, Chicago, Illinois.

Urban Planning and Land Development Control, Hagman's Hornbook on, 1971, 706 pages, by Donald G. Hagman, Professor of Law, University of California, Los Angeles.

HORNBOOKS & BASIC TEXTS

Uniform Commercial Code, White and Summers' Hornbook on, 2nd Ed., 1980, 1250 pages, by James J. White, Professor of Law, University of Michigan and Robert S. Summers, Professor of Law, Cornell University.

Wills, Atkinson's Hornbook on, 2nd Ed., 1953, 975 pages, by Thomas E. Atkinson, Late Professor of Law, New York University.

Advisory Board

LEGAL WRITING
IN A NUTSHELL

By

LYNN B. SQUIRES, Ph.D.
Legal Writing Associate
School of Law, University of Washington

MARJORIE DICK ROMBAUER
Professor of Law
School of Law, University of Washington

ST. PAUL, MINN.
WEST PUBLISHING CO.
1982

COPYRIGHT © 1982 By WEST PUBLISHING CO.
                     50 West Kellogg Boulevard
                     P.O. Box 3526
                     St. Paul, Minnesota 55165

Library of Congress Cataloging in Publication Data

Squires, Lynn B.
  Legal Writing in a nutshell.

  (Nutshell series)
  Bibliography: p.
  Includes index.
    1. Legal composition. 2. Law—United States—
Language. I. Rombauer, Marjorie Dick. II. Title.
III. Series.
KF250.S68   808'.06634021   82–7082
                                AACR2

ISBN 0-314-65346-5

      S. & R. Legal Writing, NS
      1st Reprint—1982

PREFACE

This *Nutshell* reflects the combined efforts of a law professor and a writing specialist. Professor Rombauer has been the primary author of Chapters 1 and 2, the glossary in Chapter 5, and the discussions of memoranda and features of briefs in Chapters 6 and 7. Dr. Squires has been the primary author of Chapters 3, 4, and 8 and of the other sections of Chapters 5, 6, and 7. As a result of discussion and reciprocal editing, however, the text represents a blending of the thinking and writing methods of our respective disciplines.

The unfootnoted *Nutshell* style precludes the many acknowledgements of sources that would ordinarily appear in a legal text. Therefore, we acknowledge here that most of the books included in the Selected References list appearing at the end of the text have either been consulted during the writing of this text or have shaped some part of our thinking about writing.

We are indebted to several teachers and lawyers who have read various drafts of all chapters. Most particularly, we are indebted to William F. Irmscher, Professor of English, Director of Freshman English, and Chairman of Teacher Preparation Programs at the University of Washington. Professor Irmscher read and commented extensively on most of the text. We are doubly indebted to him, since he also authored one of the frequently consulted texts included in our Selected References, *The Holt Guide to English*, as well as another source of inspiration, *Teaching Expository Writing* (1979).

Others who have read and commented on substantial portions of drafts, to whom we here express our thanks, include Ronald M. Gould, Stew Cogan, and Richard A. Derham, all lawyers practicing in Seattle, Washington; Geoffrey Crooks, Commissioner for the Supreme Court of the State of Washington; and Professor Linda S. Hume and Acting Assistant Professor Helen L. Halpert of the University of Washington School of Law.

Early versions of this *Nutshell* were used and evaluated by several first-year classes of students at the University of Washington School of Law and by associates in two Seattle firms, Perkins, Coie, Stone, Olsen, and Williams and Davis, Wright, Todd, Riese, and Jones. We here thank all those students and lawyers who used and commented on earlier drafts of this *Nutshell*.

We are grateful for permission to quote from *Corbin on Contracts*, Copyright 1965 by West Publishing Company.

Finally, we express thanks to our secretary, Li Finley, and to Jeri Miles and William Herman, who typed the manuscript.

MARJORIE DICK ROMBAUER
LYNN B. SQUIRES

Seattle, Washington
March 1982

SUMMARY OF CONTENTS

*

OUTLINE

CHAPTER 3.   SMALL–SCALE ORGANIZATION: PARAGRAPHS, PARAGRAPH BLOCKS, AND TRANSITIONS

CHAPTER 5. LANGUAGE IN THE LEGAL SETTING

CHAPTER 6. THE TOTAL PRODUCT: ADVISORY LETTERS TO LAY PERSONS; OFFICE RESEARCH MEMORANDA

CHAPTER 7. THE TOTAL PRODUCT: APPELLATE BRIEFS AND ARGU-MENTATIVE MEMORANDA

CHAPTER 8. PUNCTUATION, GRAMMAR, AND MECHANICS

OUTLINE

*

LEGAL WRITING
IN A NUTSHELL

*

INTRODUCTION

When a client's welfare is at stake, no lawyer can afford to rely on writing that clouds communication or gives the wrong impression. Disorganized writing or ambiguous sentences can conceal intended meaning; a misused word or a grammatical error can stop or slow the reader's progress. If such errors do not interfere with comprehension, they may still signal incompetence to an intelligent and demanding reader. Observance of the suggestions collected in this *Nutshell* may help to avoid either result.

Most legal writing handbooks or guides agree on the principles of good writing. This *Nutshell* collects those principles and others, as well as information that is customarily found only in English composition handbooks and style manuals. Recent research findings from the fields of composition and readability form the basis for many of the suggestions offered throughout this book.

This *Nutshell* is designed to be used both as a textbook and as a handbook during the writing process. The first chapter introduces the major forms of legal writing. The second chapter offers principles for large-scale organization of a legal memorandum or brief. The third chapter describes small-scale organization, particularly paragraphs, paragraph blocks, and transitions. The fourth chapter offers suggestions for sentence construction and for revision of sentences. The fifth includes an introduction to legal language and a glossary of words commonly misused in legal writing. Building on the descriptions and suggestions of the first five chapters, Chapters 6 and 7 provide more detailed descriptions of advisory and argumentative writing. The eighth chapter covers punctuation, grammar, and mechanics in a form useful to legal writers.

This *Nutshell* is not a complete guide to legal writing. Choices for inclusion or omission have had to be made. To compensate for the necessary omissions, the list of Selected References provided at the end supplies references to texts that deal with major subjects not discussed in the *Nutshell* as well as subjects that are covered.

Writing, including legal writing, is an art as well as a skill. The skilled legal writer who is also an artist is one who has learned when special considerations require variation from general principles. As you gain experience in legal writing, you will find that rules should sometimes be broken—if you have a good reason and know what you are doing. With experience, you will develop an individual style of writing suitable to your field of expertise.

CHAPTER 1

PURPOSES AND FORMS OF LEGAL WRITING

§ 1.1 INTRODUCTION

Some basic forms of legal writing are introduced in this chapter to provide a framework for discussion in following chapters.

The forms emphasized in this *Nutshell* can be divided into two groups:

Advisory Writing

Memoranda written for lawyers

Letters written for clients (usually persons who are not law-trained)

Argumentative Writing

Memoranda and briefs for courts, administrative agencies, arbitrators, and so on

Petitions for review, such as a Petition for Certiorari

These forms of legal writing have been chosen for description and discussion primarily because they are the forms most commonly first assigned to law students and new lawyers.

The guidelines for effective advisory and argumentative writing presented in this *Nutshell* can also be applied to these other forms of legal writing:

> That body of writing comprising our law, for example, judicial and administrative agency opinions, constitutions, statutes, regulations, ordinances, and court rules

> Scholarly forms, such as texts or law review articles, comments, notes, and book reviews

> Documents used in litigation, for example, pleading and discovery documents

> Private law documents, such as contracts, leases, trust agreements, and wills

In particular, the suggestions for effective advisory and argumentative writing can be applied to scholarly and judicial writing. The content of all these forms of writing is similar: all discuss solutions to legal problems. The writers' specific purposes will differ, however, according to the balance of their desires to inform, to predict, and to persuade.

No attempt is made to discuss examinations, the first form of legal writing prospective lawyers are required to do. Examination questions are, however, often cast in the form of legal problems that require an advisory or argumentative response. Observance of suggestions in this

Nutshell should therefore aid in developing an effective writing style for examinations.

§ 1.2 LAW OFFICE MEMORANDUM

A law office memorandum is customarily prepared for another lawyer. Its purpose is to discuss a legal problem and to suggest possible solutions or outcomes. Following are brief descriptions of the purpose and content of the sections of a standard law office memorandum form.

Title: States the title of a pending action or the name or other identification of the client whose problem is analyzed.

Requested by: (or, To:)

Submitted by: (or, From:)

Date Submitted:

Question(s) Presented

Identifies the legal issues presented by the action or problem and thus informs readers of the general content and facilitates filing of the memorandum for future reference. If key facts are so numerous that incorporation of them in the question is awkward, a brief summary of those facts may precede the question(s).

Brief Answer

Provides a specific answer to each question presented with a brief, general summary of the reasons for the answer, thus providing a quick answer for a reader who may not immediately read the detailed explanations and conclusions that follow.

Statement of Facts

Succinctly organizes and summarizes the legally significant facts of the case or problem.

Applicable Statutes

Quotes the significant portions of constitutional provisions, statutes, regulations, or other written law.

Discussion

Provides an explanation of the question(s) presented and a full explanation of the writer's analysis of the problem, authorities, rationales, and other bases for the answer(s).

Conclusion

Summarizes the writer's conclusion and advice in only slightly greater detail than is provided in the Brief Answer.

Signature

A memorandum may conclude, "Respectfully submitted," with the writer's signature, or simply with the writer's signature.

§ 1.3 ARGUMENTATIVE MEMORANDUM FORM

A written argument prepared for a trial judge (for example, in support of a motion) or for another decision maker, such as an arbitrator, may also be called a memorandum. The "memorandum" title may also be used for a motion argument or other preliminary argument prepared for an appellate court. In either situation, the content and purpose (to persuade) will be similar to the content and purpose of an appellate brief, described in a following section. Because of different prospective audiences, however, the style and level of formality may differ. Governing court rules may state special requirements. Customs of practice in a particular jurisdiction or locality may also affect form and style.

§ 1.4 LETTERS FOR CLIENTS

Letters for clients range in form from a one-paragraph request for payment of fees to a formal opinion similar in content and style to a law office memorandum. In this *Nutshell* only informal letters, for which there is no standard form, will be discussed.

§ 1.5 APPELLATE BRIEF FORM

Argumentative briefs are prepared for courts and for administrative and other tribunals. Rules for the tribunal before which an appeal or

other form of review is pending will state exact
requirements for brief form.   Although these
rule requirements differ from jurisdiction to jurisdiction, some requirements are common to all jurisdictions.   The following descriptions of the
purpose and content of the sections required by
United States Supreme Court Rule on Appeal 34
(effective June 30, 1980) for appellant's briefs on
the merits include some of those common requirements.   Some or all of the sections, and possibly
other sections, will be required for briefs on the
merits prepared for other tribunals.

The Supreme Court form is used for illustrative
purposes only, since most attorneys will not have
occasion to prepare a brief for that Court.   Controlling rules should be consulted and followed
exactly.   Failure to conform to the rules may result in delay or may even preclude review by the
tribunal.

Questions Presented

States the legal issues to be argued.   In some
state court briefs, a section on "Assignments
of Error" or "Points and Authorities" is required in addition to or instead of Questions
Presented. "Assignments" state the rulings or
other procedural actions of the lower court that
are alleged to be erroneous and that form the
basis for appeal or other review. "Points" are
summary statements of counsel's contentions,

also used as headings within the text of the argument.

Parties to Proceeding

Lists all parties for whose judgment review is sought. Not necessary if all such parties are listed in either the caption of the case or a footnote.

Table of Contents

Required for all documents filed with the United States Supreme Court that exceed five pages, unless the document contains only one item. Indexed in the table will be each of the sections described here and the headings used for the text of the argument.

Table of Authorities

Required for all documents filed with the United States Supreme Court that exceed three pages. Contains a listing of cases (alphabetically arranged), constitutional provisions, statutes, textbooks, and other authorities, with correct references to pages where cited.

Opinions and Judgments Below

Lists citations to opinions and judgments delivered by lower courts.

Jurisdictional Grounds

States grounds on which the jurisdiction of the Court is invoked and cites to the statutory provisions and to time limits on which the jurisdiction rests.

Constitutional and Other Provisions

Quotes any applicable constitutional provisions, treaties, statutes, ordinances, or regulations. If lengthy, the provisions may be cited in this section and quoted in full in an appendix to the brief.

Statement of the Case

Contains all information about the procedure and facts of the case that are material to consideration of questions presented. The rule requires appropriate references to the record of proceedings in the court below or to the joint appendix (a short form of record permitted by United States Supreme Court rules).

Summary of Argument

A suitably paragraphed, succinct condensation of arguments actually presented in the brief. Repetition of headings used in the brief does not suffice.

The Argument

Rule 34.1(i) requires that the argument clearly exhibit "the points of fact and of law being presented, citing the authorities and statutes relied upon." The contents will be similar to the Discussion in a Law Office Memorandum. The purpose is to persuade, however, and the audience may dictate different style and organization.

Conclusion

Specifies with particularity the relief requested. May briefly summarize the argument.

Signature

A brief concludes with "Respectfully submitted," and counsel's name.

An appellee's brief on the merits will include the same pages and sections with the following exceptions: A statement of the case need include only information that is necessary to correct inaccuracies or omissions in the statement by the petitioner or appellant. It need not include a statement of questions or the sections that list the parties, cite lower court opinions, state jurisdictional grounds, and quote constitutional and other provisions.

A brief filed by an *amicus curiae* (friend of the court) is sufficient if it includes a statement of the nature of the writer's interest, the summary of argument, the argument, and the conclusion. The Court's permission to file is required for an *amicus* brief unless all parties consent to the filing.

§ 1.6 PETITIONS FOR REVIEW

If review of a decision by a higher tribunal is not required by controlling law but is discretion-

ary with that tribunal, some form of petition for
review will be required. The purpose of such a
petition (to persuade the tribunal to accept review
of the matter and schedule it for consideration on
the merits) will be similar to the purpose of argumentative memoranda and briefs. The form and
contents may also be substantially similar. For
example, United States Supreme Court Rule on
Appeal 21 requires that a petition for a writ of
certiorari shall contain essentially the same pages
and sections as are required by Rule 34 for briefs
on the merits, in addition to material particularly
relevant to the preliminary character of the petition.

CHAPTER 2

LARGE–SCALE ORGANIZATION

§ 2.1 INTRODUCTION

All writing must be organized on several levels. Even a one-sentence statute must have a structure—an order of parts that communicates a thought rather than a jumble of words, phrases, and clauses. The larger the unit of writing, the more levels on which the writing must be organized. Thus, sentences must be arranged within paragraphs. Paragraphs must be arranged in paragraph blocks to present larger units of thought. In extended writings, paragraph blocks and other individual paragraphs must then be arranged within sections and the sections presented in a rational order for the final whole. The organization at each level will reflect relationships between different parts of the whole.

Larger units of organization are discussed in this chapter. Emphasis is on the overall framework of comprehensive advisory and argumentative writings and the larger units within that framework.

[*13*]

§ 2.2   BASIC PRINCIPLES OF ORGANIZATION

Appropriate organization for a large piece of writing will depend on such special considerations as the form and type of writing, its purpose, the subject matter, and the person to whom it is addressed (the "audience"). Nevertheless, a few basic principles can be followed unless those special considerations suggest different organizing principles. The basic principles are stated in this section. Ways in which the special considerations may affect these basic principles are then discussed in the following sections.

(a) Introduce, Explain, Conclude

Both objective and argumentative legal writings should normally follow the traditional forensic pattern: they should introduce what will be said, say it, and then summarize what was said. This pattern should also be used within sections of an extended writing.

(b) Put Essential Things First

Whatever the form or purpose of a legal writing, it should deal first with the essentials, those matters that are necessary to an understanding of what follows. In the following example, the

[*14*]

essential governing principles are stated first to introduce discussion of a problem.

A contract entered into under duress may be avoided by a person who acted under duress. *See generally Restatement of Contracts* §§ 494–495 (1932). Modern authorities agree that a good faith threat of criminal prosecution may be the basis for finding that duress induced a person to enter into a contract. *See generally Restatement of Contracts* § 493 and Comment b (1932); 13 *Williston on Contracts* §§ 1611–15 (3d ed. W. Jaeger 1970). The primary questions presented in our client's case stem from the Washington court's inconsistency in considering whether such a threat may constitute duress as a matter of law.

Factual considerations as well as legal principles may be essentials when, for example, the resolution of a problem will ultimately turn on the resolution of a factual question or the result of future investigations.

The crucial question in this case is whether our client promised to arrange for transfer of the fire insurance policy covering the warehouse sold to the plaintiffs. If a promise was made, two theories may support a recovery for the plaintiff. The testimony of the lender's attorney, the only disinterested witness, will probably be more favorable to the plaintiff than to our client on this question. The following discussion is therefore based on an assumption that a judge or jury would find that a promise had been made.

Putting essential matters first is important to maintain reader interest as well as to aid reader understanding. The legal writer must get to the essentials quickly or risk losing the reader's attention. This is true whether that reader is a judge, a law clerk, a client, or another lawyer.

(c) Keep Related Matters Together

Order of presentation can suggest relationships indirectly, even though the relationships are not expressly stated. It can also reinforce explicit statements about relationships. Therefore, a large part of deciding on appropriate organization is identifying the relationships to be communicated. After relationships are identified, an organization that keeps related matters together should be planned.

(d) Use Headings and Transitions

Headings and subheadings are necessary aids to keep the reader informed of subject matter changes. Topic headings should be used for major divisions. Subheadings may be used to identify the topic of a paragraph or block of paragraphs. In addition to headings, explicit transitions should be included to guide the reader from point to point and from question to question. These may be transitional words, sentences or paragraphs. See the section on transitions in Chapter 3.

[*16*]

§ 2.3 ORGANIZATION OF ADVISORY AND ARGUMENTATIVE WRITING

Both advisory and argumentative writing consist of several basic ingredients: facts, questions, authorities, rules, rationales, applications, and conclusions. These ingredients shape the organization of the basic forms of legal writing introduced in Chapter 1. For example, compare the following outlines for standard law office memorandum form and for United States Supreme Court brief form. (Some preliminary sections are omitted as not relevant to the immediate discussion.)

Memoranda	*Briefs*
Questions Presented	Questions Presented
Brief Answer	Constitutional and Other Provisions
Statement of Facts	Statement of Case
Applicable Statutes (or other written law)	Summary of Argument
Discussion	Argument
Conclusion	Conclusion

Note that the order is the same for the key sections: questions, facts, discussion/argument, and conclusion.

§ 2.4   ORGANIZATION OF DISCUSSION OR ARGUMENT SECTIONS

(a) Introduction

The heart of advisory writing is the Discussion section, and the heart of argumentative writing is the Argument section. In these sections, the questions presented will be restated and explained; relevant authorities will be cited and discussed; policies, rules, and rationales will be examined and applied to the significant facts; and specific conclusions will be stated.

If a problem or case presents more than one question, the order in which the Questions Presented and subquestions are stated will provide the basic framework. Therefore, the first decision about organization is the appropriate order of discussion for the questions. The following principles and examples provide some guidelines for that decision. The examples are taken from law office memoranda only. If the goal is to persuade, as in an appellate brief, these organizational patterns may be altered for rhetorical effect. (See Chapter 7.)

(b) Interdependent or Other Logical Order

(1) Interdependent Questions

Sometimes the existence of a question or the answer to a question will depend on the answer to another question. Discussion of the prior question first will usually make the interrelationship easier for the reader to understand and will avoid awkward cross-referencing.

Our client sold a warehouse that was later destroyed by fire. The buyer, Emory, alleges that at the time the sale was closed, our client promised to arrange for transfer of his fire insurance policy for the benefit of the buyer.

Question: May the client be liable to the buyer for the full loss for failing to perform the alleged promise?

1. Did our client promise Emory to arrange for transfer of the insurance policy? (fact question)

2. Assuming that our client did so promise, was the promise sufficiently definite to be enforceable?

3. Assuming that a sufficiently definite promise was made, would the parol evidence rule make evidence of the oral promise inadmissible, or would the exception for subsequent or separate agreements apply?

4. If evidence of the oral promise is admissible, would the promise be enforceable without Emory having given or promised consideration for it?

[*19*]

    a.   Would the promise be enforceable under the promissory estoppel doctrine?

    b.   Would a promissory duty be enforced under the *Hudson* gratuitous agency rule?

(2) Chronological Order

If questions are related to a chronology of events, discussion in the order in which events occurred will often facilitate understanding.

EXAMPLE 1:

A.   Did our client, Lewis, tortiously induce Dunlap to breach a contract for exchange of his boat for Tyler's boat?

    1.   Did a valid contract exist between Tyler and Dunlap at the time Lewis first discussed trading his boat for Dunlap's boat on September 15th, or had the Tyler-Dunlap contract already been breached by repudiation on September 14th?

    2.   Assuming that a valid contract did exist on September 15th, did Lewis's conduct in offering to exchange his boat on similar terms, making disparaging remarks about Tyler's boat, and contracting with Dunlap for exchange of their boats constitute the kind of interference that may be the basis for a tort action?

    3.   Was Lewis's conduct privileged because he was a "competitor"?

B.   Did Lewis's conduct in taking Dunlap's boat from Tyler's dock on September 18th induce or cause termination of a valid business expectancy?

EXAMPLE 2:

A. Must evidence of remarriage of a plaintiff in a wrongful death action be excluded as irrelevant?

B. Even though such evidence would otherwise be excluded,

    1. Can questions about plaintiff's new spouse be asked during *voir dire* to ascertain prospective jurors' possible acquaintance with the new spouse?

    2. Can questions about the plaintiff's continued use of her prior name be asked on cross-examination to attack her credibility?

(3) Authority Value Order

Ordinarily, questions governed by different forms of law should be discussed in the order of the authority value of the form: constitutional questions should be discussed first, then statutory questions, and then common law questions, because constitutional provisions would ordinarily override statutory provisions, and statutory provisions would ordinarily override prior common law. This order may be altered, however, by the source of a question. For example, a possible interpretation of a statute may create a constitutional question, requiring that the statutory interpretation question be discussed first. The same change in order may be suggested by courts' preference to avoid constitutional questions if a possible interpretation of a statute might make decision of the constitutional question unnecessary. Also, the need to determine the meaning of a common law concept incorporated in a statute may require that common law precedents defining the concept be discussed first.

Interwoven with the order suggested by forms of law may be the order suggested by levels of governmental source of authority. Thus, federal questions and authorities would ordinarily be discussed first, then state questions and authorities, and then authorities from lower governmental units.

Intermixed with both the form and source of authority may be another hierarchy of authority, that is, mandatory and persuasive sources (for common law questions, for example) and secondary sources. If, however, mandatory authorities are not directly in point and persuasive or secondary authorities are, then this order, too, may be altered.

(4) Conceptual or Rule Element Order

Statutory and other rules may incorporate several elements that must be established before the statute or rule can be said to govern resolution of a particular problem. If questions are presented for more than one such element, discussion in the order the elements appear in the statute or rule may be the appropriate order. For example, the federal Anti-kickback Act, 41 U. S. C. § 51 (1976), states a series of requirements for recovery by the government of certain kickbacks: a payment made "on behalf of" a subcontractor, to certain representatives of a primary contractor holding a "negotiated contract," "as an inducement" for the award of a subcontract or order, and so forth. If questions about each of the quoted phrases were presented, the order in which they appear in the statute might be an appropriate order of discussion.

(c) Order of Importance

Order of "importance" will be influenced by the particular writing task. In a brief, the strongest argument will usually be the most "important." In a memorandum prepared to help an attorney decide whether to institute litigation, the weakest link may be the most "important." Ultimately, you will find that decisions about the relative importance of ideas or arguments must be based on thorough understanding of the substance of particular problems. No general writing principles can guide you in making such decisions.

(d) Order of Request

If you have been asked to discuss particular questions, and if those questions have no natural order or variation in importance, then follow the order suggested in the request. Such requests may come from another attorney (as for a law office memorandum) or from a judge (as for a memorandum on evidentiary questions that have arisen during the trial).   If the request comes from a judge, strategies for persuasion may suggest a different order.   (See Chapter 7.)

§ 2.5   PRINCIPLES OF ORGANIZATION FOR INDIVIDUAL QUESTIONS

(a) Use Basic Analytical Organization Absent Special Considerations

For each Question Presented, there is a predetermined analytical content for discussion or argument: The question will be stated and explained; authorities will be cited and discussed; rules, rationales, and policies will be explained and applied to the significant facts; and specific conclusions will be expressed.   This predetermined content also suggests an organization for discussion of each question.   Prefaced by statement of the answer, this analytical organization can be used unless special considerations suggest some variation.

The suggested organization is illustrated in the following discussion of a simple legal question. For more difficult questions, each part may require its own paragraph or block of paragraphs.

Conclusion

Specific question and answer

Authorities

Our client did not tortiously induce breach of the Tyler-Dunlap contract. The basic question is whether a contract that has been consistently repudiated by the maker (as by Dunlap in this case) is the kind of contractual relationship protected by the tortious interference rule. It is not. See *Restatement (Second) of Torts* § 766, Comment f (1979); *United States v. Newbury Mfg. Co.*, 36 F. Supp. 602 (D.Mass.1941).

In *Newbury*, the United States had entered into a contract with Defendant Newbury and had delivered goods that Newbury had agreed to dispose of by export to foreign countries only. The United States alleged a breach by Newbury in contracting to sell the goods to Defendant Belmont *and others* in the United States. It also alleged tortious interference by Belmont in inducing breach. In granting Belmont's motion to dismiss for failure to state a claim, the court held that Belmont could not be held liable for tortious interference, stating in part,

Rationale

36 F.Supp. at 605: "The rule [respecting recovery for tortious interference] presupposes that the party defaulting was ready, able, and willing to perform and would have done so if it had not been prevented or persuaded by the malicious and un-

warranted interference of a third party."

Application to facts   In our client's case, Dunlap had failed and refused to perform his contract with Tyler continuously for at least thirteen days before our client allegedly interfered. Therefore, *Restatement of conclusion* Tyler did not have the kind of contractual relationship contemplated by the rule against interference, and our client could not tortiously induce breach of the Tyler-Dunlap contract.

Although the suggested analytical organization is often sufficient, special considerations may suggest variation. For example, if authorities are weak and policy considerations are strong, policy should be discussed before authorities under the principle that the more important matter should appear first. Then, too, not all questions require discussion of each part included in the example, while many questions require discussion of other types of content (for example, fact questions that must be discussed before a rule is applied to the significant facts).

(b) Begin With Statement of Your Answer Absent Special Considerations

One feature of the organization suggested in the preceding subsection should usually not be varied: Statement of a specific answer to a Question Presented should ordinarily not be deferred beyond the beginning point. Two reasons dictate this highlighting of conclusions. First, advisory writing is intended to inform as the basis for advice, and argumentative writing is intended to lead another's thinking as the basis for persuasion. Knowing where a discussion or argument is leading is essential if a reader is to be informed or persuaded. Second, knowing where a discussion or argument is leading is essential if a reader is to understand on first reading. A reader's understanding on first reading is a significant objective for this kind of writing because the reader will almost always want to grasp the material in minimum reading time. In some circumstances, the reader may be required to understand on the basis of scanning rather than careful reading. You should not ordinarily expect your reader to return to a preliminary Brief Answer or Summary of Argument in order to have your conclusions in mind. Neither should your reader have to look ahead to the formal, summarizing Conclusion to determine where you are leading.

Special circumstances may require that statement of an answer be deferred. For example, if you are not sure that your reader understands the subject area about which you are writing, you should provide a background introduction. Similarly, you may need to explain why a question is presented if that is not evident.

§ 2.6 IS AN OUTLINE NECESSARY?

The purpose and form of advisory and argumentative writing will provide a general framework. Must you identify a more detailed structure before you begin writing?

Many writing experts emphatically recommend that writers prepare a formal, detailed outline before beginning to write. Experienced legal writers do not always follow that recommendation. Sometimes they produce a readable product nevertheless. Sometimes—at least as often—they produce a product that is disorganized or incomprehensible. The different results are explainable.

Often a written outline is unnecessary because the writer has a sufficient outline in mind. Perhaps the writer understands the subject very well; perhaps the subject is very simple or the subject matter has an inherent structure; perhaps the writer's notes (research notes, for example) are so neat and well structured as to shape the mental outline. In any event, the writer *is* following a predetermined outline of some sort.

Alternatively, a writer may begin writing with the expectation of developing appropriate structure in the writing process. This approach, too, may ultimately produce a good product. Trying to express one's thoughts may lead to new thoughts. New viewpoints, new syntheses, new

[*28*]

relationships may be recognized. A continuing interaction between the process of writing and the writing itself may lead to recognition of a structure that was not recognized at the beginning. Once an appropriate structure is recognized, the process should be reversed. An outline of the draft, reorganized and filled out with additional details, can then be the starting point for a less tentative draft.

Note, however, that writing in search of structure can be a time-consuming process—and may be an unproductive process. The answer to the question of whether to outline, therefore, is, "Yes, you should try to write an outline if you do not have a clear mental outline of a well understood, simple, or inherently structured subject." Attempting to outline can also lead to recognition of structure. More importantly, attempting to write an outline can lead to a clearer view of what you want to say.

Therefore, plan to begin advisory or argumentative writing by outlining at least a general framework. Then add as many details as your immediate understanding of the subject permits. Do not feel committed to forcing everything into a highly structured outline (that is, in complete sentences, neatly ordered under an appropriate combination of Roman numerals, capital letters, and so on). Outlining is an efficient prewriting exercise as long as your approach remains flexible. The need for details grows, however, as the complexity of the subject increases. Paradoxically, the greater the prospective writer's uncertainty about the subject, the greater the need to push the search for structure.

Use of a dictating machine makes outlining more important. Preparing an outline of main points and key phrases before dictating will save editorial and revision time later.

§ 2.7   ILLUSTRATIVE GENERAL OUTLINE

The following general outline of a memorandum discussion is provided to demonstrate some of the organization principles discussed in this chapter. The order of discussion for each question might be altered by one or more other organizational considerations. For example, if the answer to the statutory question will determine whether there is a constitutional question, the statutory question might be discussed first. An outline for an argument addressed to the same questions might be varied for reasons of persuasion as discussed in Chapter 7.

Background explanation of subject area of problem
Statement of ultimate conclusion
First question (assume a constitutional question)
　Statement of conclusion
　Discussion of authority
　　Language of constitution

Construing court opinions (discussion of holdings, dicta, underlying rules, rationales, and policies)

Supreme Court, circuit court of appeal

State appellate courts, federal district courts

Secondary authorities

Supporting or countervailing policy considerations

Application to facts

Restatement of conclusion

Second question (assume a statutory question)

Explanation of statutory language that creates the question

Statement of conclusion

Discussion of authority

Legislative history

Construing court opinions

Application to facts

Restatement of conclusion

Third question (assume a common law question)

Statement of conclusion

Explanation why question is presented

Discussion of authorities

Mandatory precedents (discussion of holdings, dicta, underlying rules, and rationales of the courts of the jurisdiction whose law controls)

Policy considerations

Persuasive authorities (discussion of holdings, dicta and so on from courts of other jurisdictions)

Secondary authorities

Conclusion (summarizing and relating the answers to the individual questions and restating the ultimate conclusion)

CHAPTER 3

SMALL–SCALE ORGANIZATION: PARAGRAPHS, PARAGRAPH BLOCKS, AND TRANSITIONS

§ 3.1 INTRODUCTION

Small-scale organization is the ordering of smaller units within sections of, for example, a memorandum or brief. These smaller units are paragraphs or paragraph blocks, joined by transitions. A paragraph block is several paragraphs that develop a single, major topic. In this chapter, the basic principles of paragraph organization will be summarized, followed by a discussion of paragraph blocks. The chapter concludes with a review of transitional devices.

§ 3.2 BASIC PRINCIPLES OF PARAGRAPH ORGANIZATION

(a) Introduction

Just as overall organization of a discussion or argument communicates meaning, so does paragraph structure. Readers expect, for example, that a paragraph will have a governing theme (a "topic") and that the first sentence in the paragraph will state the topic. This expectation parallels the standard paragraph pattern: The topic sentence, usually the first, introduces the paragraph theme; the remaining sentences elaborate on it. In longer paragraphs, the final sentence may recapitulate the theme or offer a conclusion.

While we as readers look for the standard paragraph pattern, as writers we do not always provide it. Most writers paragraph intuitively, basing their decisions to break on a sense of closure. Most of the time, a good writer's intuition will result in clear and meaningful paragraph divisions. Good writers will have more control and more consistent success, however, if they understand the principles that they intuitively observe.

We paragraph for several reasons: (i) for logical divisions (for example, separation of issues or case analyses), (ii) for rhetorical purposes, and (iii) for visual effect. These often overlap. In legal writing, paragraphing normally should reflect logical divisions. Much of legal writing consists of the development of an argument or of analysis of an issue through logical steps. Those steps make up individual paragraphs while the argument as a whole makes up a block of paragraphs.

Like punctuation in general, paragraphing is a matter of desired effect as well as of interpretation. A series of long paragraphs, for example, invites a short one for contrast and emphasis, and

[*34*]

a series of short paragraphs invites a single expansive one.

(b) Use Meaningful Paragraph Blocks

Paragraph blocks in legal writing are usually more important structural divisions than individual paragraphs. Traditional discussions of paragraphing are therefore inadequate for the legal writer who must organize groups of paragraphs into sections and subsections of memoranda and briefs. The commonplace Issue-Rule-Application-Conclusion ("IRAC") paragraph pattern described below, for example, typically requires a block of two or more paragraphs and only rarely can be managed in a single paragraph. Similarly, the comparison and contrast paragraph pattern used to analyze facts in a series of cases generally requires several paragraphs.

Paragraph blocks are groups of paragraphs that together present a major point. They may consist of two or of a dozen or more paragraphs. They may fall under a single subheading, or several blocks may fall under the same subheading. A heading identifying the theme of the block is customary and helpful.

A paragraph block often begins with a paragraph introducing the theme or topic of the block. The following paragraphs then develop that theme. The paragraph block is thus frequently an expansion of the standard pattern: the standard topic sentence expanded into a paragraph, the supporting sentences into separate paragraphs, and the concluding sentence expanded into a concluding paragraph. This expansion allows for a more detailed discussion of substance without interminable paragraphs.

The legal writer may not need to plan such paragraph blocks in advance. A block of related paragraphs will develop during the writing process. After a draft is completed, however, the writer should check to see if the paragraph pattern will be intelligible to the reader. That is, the writer should identify (perhaps by outlining roughly) the paragraph blocks, check for a governing major theme, and check transitions between component paragraphs.

Although legal writers need not design paragraph blocks in advance or attempt to construct them while writing, they should work consciously to link inner parts, that is, to tie paragraphs together. Identifying transitional elements is part of the analytical task of the legal writer; such elements are essential for a reader's comprehension.

(c) Avoid Excesses in Paragraph Length

Within a paragraph block, a paragraph is a mark of punctuation. Like the period, the last sentence of a paragraph marks closure of a theme. The theme of a paragraph must be one that can be stated, developed, and closed within a unit of writing long enough to hold interest but short enough to be read and understood as a unit. If a reader must reread a paragraph to grasp the theme, then the paragraph is too long. If a paragraph or series of paragraphs presents a chopped-up theme, then the paragraphs are too short. No mechanical rule can provide a guide for the writer to know when a paragraph is "too long" or "too short." If a paragraph is longer than half a standard 250-word page, consider dividing it. Remember that readers appreciate the mental break that a new paragraph provides.

(d) Use One-or Two-Sentence Paragraphs Sparingly

Just as the very short sentence lends emphasis to a point, so a single-sentence paragraph lends emphasis to its content. Such paragraphs should be used sparingly for special effect. They may highlight a major transition, emphasize an important conclusion, or summarize a block of paragraphs.

(e) Use the First and Last Sentences as Positions of Emphasis

The most important ideas should appear in the first and last sentences of a paragraph. These

sentences will usually be the more general statements, with more detailed ones in the middle of
the paragraph.

(f) Avoid Placing Full Citations in the Positions of Emphasis

Because the first and last sentences are positions of greatest emphasis within a paragraph, to
clutter them with long citations is to distract
from the point. Note how the citation delays attention to the substance of the following
sentences.

> In *Allen v. Ennis*, 253 App.Div. 769, 300 N.Y.S.2d
> 1323 (3d Dept. 1937), a commission employee of the
> defendant automobile dealer negligently caused the
> death of the passenger while demonstrating a car.
> He was convicted of negligent homicide despite his
> lack of actual knowledge of the car defect that con-
> tributed to the fatal accident. His status as an em-
> ployee did not alter his responsibility to be aware of
> the limitations of the vehicle that he was driving.

When an authority is the theme of a paragraph,
as in the *Allen v. Ennis* paragraph, the writer
should attempt to characterize the authority by
subject matter, source, or other significant detail.
Then the citation may be stated as a separate sentence or as the last part of the topic sentence.

> *Revision of the above example:* In another negli-
> gent homicide prosecution [or, In a New York case,
> or, In an early case] a commission employee of the
> defendant automobile dealer had negligently caused

the death of the passenger while demonstrating a car. *Allen v. Ennis,* 253 App.Div. 769, 300 N.Y.S.2d 1323 (3d Dept. 1937). [Note the treatment of this separate citation as a sentence by use of a period at the end.]

§ 3.3 STANDARD PARAGRAPH AND PARAGRAPH BLOCK PATTERNS

(a) TEC Pattern: Topic Sentence, Elaboration, Conclusion

In the standard paragraph, the first sentence introduces or signals the topic. If you cannot summarize the topic or subject of a paragraph in a single sentence, then you are including too much in the paragraph. The topic sentence is customarily followed by supporting discussion: illustration, example, analysis, or explanation. A conclusion may or may not end the paragraph.

Topic sentences stating a legal proposition:

1. "Willful" means more than merely involuntary action.

2. A prior restraint regulation must contain precise criteria, spelling out what is forbidden.

Topic sentences phrased as direct or indirect questions:

1. Did the court have jurisdiction under the general statute?

2. The question is whether the three-year or the six-year limitation should be applied.

Topic sentences phrased as conclusions.

1.   Our client will have no right to reject future deliveries if it accepts the present consignment.

2.   Our client's conduct will probably not be found to have been reasonable.

T   *Example of TEC paragraph*:   The decisional scheme of the Siting Act should not be subject to review despite the provisions of that Act for judicial review.   The scheme is similar to that held by the Su-

E   preme Court to be non-reviewable in *Chicago & Southern Air Lines, Inc. v. Waterman S. S. Corp.*, 333 U.S. 103 (1948).   In that case the Court considered a clause in the Civil Aeronautics Act that provided, as does the Siting Act, that certain orders of the Civil Aeronautics Board (CAB) were subject to the approval of the President.   The Supreme Court held that because this clause created an implied exception to the same Act that provided for judicial review of the CAB's orders, the CAB's orders were not reviewable. The Court reasoned that the President's decision, necessary to the effectiveness of the CAB's order, was political, not judicial, and hence not reviewable.   333 U.S. at 111.

C   Since the decisional scheme in the Siting Act is based on a similar clause, making approval of siting a political rather than a judicial decision, this scheme should not be subject to review.

(b) ET Pattern: Elaboration, Topic

This variation of the standard pattern provides an inductive structure: first the support or elaboration is given, then the topic. The topic statement at the end functions like a conclusion. Since this pattern leaves the reader guessing what the point will be, it should be used advisedly. One possible use is for introductory or concluding paragraphs. In an introductory paragraph, the inductive pattern allows the writer to lead the reader into a subject by using particulars that build to a generalization. This may be advantageous if the reader might otherwise find it difficult to believe the generalization or if the reader is likely to resist the generalization initially. In a concluding paragraph, the inductive pattern presents no mystery since, presumably, the reader has already comprehended the discussion or analysis that is being summarized. A summary ET paragraph may also serve as a rhetorical device to emphasize an important conclusion. In general, however, the ET or inductive pattern of paragraph development frustrates the reader, as demonstrated in the following example.

E   *ET Paragraph*: In *Kephart* a husband was convicted on the basis of his wife's testimony that he had burned a barn belonging to her. Reasoning that the governing statute adopts the common-law rule that excepts crimes of violence against the other spouse and that the arson was against the wife's

property and not against her, the court overturned the verdict and adopted the present
E   rule. In another arson case, *State v. Moxley*, the wife was allowed to testify that her husband had threatened to kill her. He returned that night and set fire to the home in which she was sleeping. The court held that the arson was a crime of personal violence against the wife. The decision turned on the fact that the arson appeared to be the husband's way of carrying out his threat. In addition, the court held that a threat could not be a confidential communication. Arson was also found to be a crime of personal violence
E   against the wife in *State v. Lammert*, 14 Wash.App. 137, 540 P.2d 466 (1975). The divorced wife was allowed to testify about acts and facts which did not involve confidential communications induced by the marital rela-
T   tion. Therefore, while courts have held in recent cases that arson can be a crime of personal violence, the courts have been careful to emphasize that no confidential communications were involved.

This paragraph is confusing because it has no clear focus. The reader must collect loosely linked ideas and remember them until the end when the point of the paragraph is finally made. No rhetorical purpose is served in this instance by the suspense.

(c) IRAC Pattern: Issue, Rule, Application of Rule to Facts, Conclusion

The basic structure for an analytical paragraph or paragraph block includes (i) the issue, (ii) the governing rules of law, (iii) relevant facts, (iv) application of law to facts, and (v) conclusion or summary of statement.

For an effective IRAC paragraph: The issue must be stated, usually in the topic sentence. The issue statement should precede statement of the rule or the governing law. An application of the rule to the facts should follow the rule or the governing law. The content of each paragraph or paragraph block should be summarized at its end.

I   Example of IRAC: The issue is whether police seizure of a presumably stolen television set can be justified under the plain view doctrine. The court has held that such seizure can be justified if an officer has
R   knowledge that the goods are stolen. In *State v. Keefe* the court found that the seizure of a typewriter that came into plain view during the proper search of Keefe's residence was unjustified. Although the officers suspected that the defendant was part of a forgery ring that made use of a typewriter, they did not have immediate knowledge that the typewriter was evidence of the crime. The court found that the typewriter was merely an item of "possible evidentiary value" and, as such, could not be the subject

A   of further search or seizure. Similarly, the television set in our case is, at best, of only "possible" evidentiary value. Since the officers did not know that the set had been sto-

C   len, the warrantless seizure of the set cannot be justified by relying on the plain view doctrine.

(d) PS Pattern: Problem, Solution

If a paragraph begins with the statement of a problem, the reader expects some indication of its solution before the paragraph closes.

P   *Example of PS*: The District needed to establish the starting and ending times of the 1976–77 student day by August 1, 1976. Without determining the duration of the student day, the District was unable to arrange course offerings and schedules, arrange and test bus routes, engage sufficient busses, notify bus drivers of route bidding, inform the public of bus routes and times, coordinate special education programs with surrounding school districts, hire and assign personnel, and so forth. The striking teachers' union was unwilling to recommence negotiations or to meet with the Board. Consequently, on

S   July 10 the Board approved the 1976–1977 student day as developed and recommended by the administration. The starting and ending times, based on many operational considerations, are shown below. (Details of Solution follow.)

[*44*]

(e) Comparison and Contrast Patterns

Legal analysis frequently requires comparisons and contrasts, that is, explanations of similarities and differences between cases, fact patterns, laws, or theories. Comparisons may be as broad as in Model One below or as narrow as in Model Three. The structure chosen should reflect the degree of detail or the fineness of analysis required by the subject matter.

Model One provides a general, not a detailed, comparison. The limitation of this model is that the reader will not remember all the points made in paragraph A while reading paragraph B.

Model One: ¶ *One (Theory A) followed by*
      ¶ *Two (Theory B)*

¶ One, Theory A

Even though the Council was not required to consider alternative sites for the power plant, it nevertheless did so, and such consideration was more than sufficient to meet any reasonable standard. The evidence on alternative sites was extensive. For example, the evidence included a comprehensive point-by-point evaluation of the Valley site in comparison with the two potential sites considered to be the next best. After weighing this evidence, the Council found that none of the alternatives was "preferable" to the Valley site. Two standards are implicit in the Council's findings: (1) that a site is satisfactory and should be approved unless it appears that another site is clearly preferable and (2) that the Council, as a licensing agency, should approve or reject a proposed site rather than select one for the applicant.

¶ Two, Theory B

Petitioners, on the other hand, would have the Council determine which site is the "best" site from among what they refer to as the "available alternative sites." They would require the Council, in each certification proceeding, to recommend rejection of the application unless it can be established that the proposed site is the best available site in the state. They would force applicants and their ratepayers to incur substantial additional costs in selecting, studying, documenting, and evaluating alternative sites. They would apply this standard to the Council's licensing action, even though the agency is empowered only to approve or reject the site proposed by the applicant. Petitioners would have the Council itself choose a site for the applicant.

Model Two requires a strong internal transition, as well as a tighter comparison of A and B. The transition is, "The Petitioners were not, however, satisfied with this finding."

Model Two: *¶ One, Theory A, then Theory B*

A   Even though the Council was not required
            to consider alternative sites for the power
            plant, it nevertheless did so. Its considera-
            tion was more than sufficient to meet any
            reasonable standard. The evidence on alter-
            native sites was extensive. For example, it
            included a comprehensive point-by-point eval-
            uation of the Valley site in comparison with
            the two potential sites considered to be the
            next best. After weighing this evidence the
            Council found that none of the alternatives
            was preferable to the Valley site. The Peti-
            tioners were not, however, satisfied with this

B   finding. Petitioners would have the Council determine which cite is the best site from among those they refer to as the "available alternative sites." They would require the Council, in each certification proceeding, to recommend rejection of the application unless it can be established that the proposed site is the best available site in the state. This would force applicants and their ratepayers to incur substantial additional costs in selecting, studying, documenting, and evaluating alternative sites. It would require a degree of precision in evaluation and comparison of sites that is presently unattainable. Thus, the Council properly rejected the "best" site standard.

In Model Three, A and B are compared on three levels or in terms of three subtopics. This model requires five transitions (as opposed to one) between A and B. It is accordingly more difficult to write but allows for more detailed comparison and contrast.

Model Three: ¶ Block, AB, AB, AB, A

A   Even though the Council was not required to consider alternative sites, it nevertheless did so. The extensive evidence collected on alternative sites included a comprehensive point-by-point evaluation of the Valley site in comparison with the two potential sites considered to be the next best. After weighing this evidence, the Council found that none of the alternatives was "preferable" to the Val-
B   ley site. Petitioners, on the other hand, would have the Council determine which site

[*47*]

is the "best" from among what they refer to as the "available alternative sites."

A   This "best site" standard would force applicants and their ratepayers to incur substantial additional costs in selecting, studying, documenting, and evaluating alternative
B   sites.   Although, as Petitioners claim, the standard requires a greater degree of precision in evaluating and comparing sites than the Council's own standard, that degree of precision is presently unattainable.

Whether or not the "best" site standard is feasible, the Council is not empowered to em-
A   ploy it.   The Council, as a licensing agency, may approve or reject a proposed site, but not select one for the applicant.   Petitioners argue that the Council is responsible for se-
B   lecting, or compelling the selection, of the best available site in the state.   The Council is empowered only to approve a satisfactory site, however, unless it appears that another site is clearly preferable.

A   Because   the   Council   has   found   no preferable alternative, there is no basis in either law or reason for the application of petitioners' "best" site standard.   Therefore, the Council's rejection of this standard is proper.

(f) Definition Pattern

This paragraph pattern consists of a detailed definition of a legal concept or area of law.   It functions like the Rule section of an IRAC paragraph.   It is more effective if preceded by a

statement of the issue in an earlier paragraph
and if followed by an application of the definition
in a subsequent paragraph.

Example of Definition Paragraph: An arrest
must be based on probable cause to be lawful. Section 12A.01.140 of the Seattle Criminal Code specifies that "a peace officer may arrest a person without a warrant if the officer has *probable cause* to
believe that such a person has committed a crime."
[emphasis supplied] Therefore, a warrantless arrest
must be carefully scrutinized to ensure that probable cause exists. *United States v. Ventresca*, 380
U.S. 102, 85 S.Ct. 741, 13 L.Ed.2d 684 (1965). The
test for probable cause is whether there is enough
information to warrant a man of reasonable caution
to believe that a crime has been committed and that
the person arrested has committed it. *Carroll v.
United States*, 267 U.S. 132, 162, 45 S.Ct. 280, 69 L.
Ed. 543 (1925). There is thus a two-part, conjunctive
requirement. The officer must have a reasonably
certain belief: (1) that a crime has been committed
and (2) that the person to be arrested has committed
it. [Next paragraph turns to application of this definition.]

§ 3.4 TRANSITIONS

(a) Introduction

A good transition refers to what has preceded
and announces what is to follow.

Without transitions, a piece of legal writing is
like a mosaic without glue: nothing, no matter
how elegantly designed, holds together. With

good transitions, even a poorly organized discussion can be understood. For substantive coherence, every sentence should be linked to its surrounding sentences. Every paragraph should be linked to the preceding paragraph, either by theme or by explicit transitional words, unless the writer has moved from one unrelated issue to another. Even then a transition may be needed to signal the lack of relationship if headings are not used.

Transitions between issues, subissues, and paragraph blocks must be carefully constructed. These may be (i) paragraphs in themselves, that is, transitional paragraphs, (ii) the first sentence in a subsequent paragraph, (iii) the last sentence in a preceding paragraph, or (iv) a substantive link between paragraphs.

(b) Transitional Paragraphs

Transitional or "roadmap" paragraphs may be used to link discussion of two issues. Issue discussions are normally separated in memoranda and briefs by major headings that provide a sharp visual break. A transitional paragraph appears at the start of discussion of the second issue or, less commonly, at the end of discussion of the first. The transitional paragraph will be effective at the end of the first issue only if the conclusion for that issue forecasts the discussion of the second issue or leads logically into it. Nor-

mally, the first paragraph of the second issue (in which the relationship between the two issues is explained) serves as the transitional paragraph.

If two questions bear no relationship to one another, then the writer should simply regard the first paragraph of the second issue as a fresh start and make no reference to the first issue. The headings and format of the memorandum or brief will provide sufficient visual division.

A transitional paragraph will usually be short. Its purpose will be to explain the relationship between two issues, subissues, or major points. If the next question to be discussed is stated at the end of a section, then the answer provided in the first paragraph of the next section will serve as an efficient transition.

A transitional paragraph may be used to summarize the content of a paragraph block and to introduce the next paragraph block. Such a paragraph calls attention to an important change of topic, to a shift in the logical sequence of ideas, to a conclusion, or perhaps to a single, telling point. When writing a paragraph meant to link two paragraph blocks, ask yourself: Why go on to the next topic? What is the next logical step?

The most effective transitional paragraphs are those in which the substantive link is clear without the aid of well-worn transitional words and phrases, such as "The next point is" or "Another important theory is."

(c) Transitional Sentences

Two successive paragraphs are most commonly linked by a transitional sentence. The writer must construct paragraphs so that either the first leads into the second or the second refers back to the first. This usually is done in a transitional sentence. An excellent transitional device from the reader's point of view is a sentence summarizing the preceding paragraph. For example, this summary sentence might link two paragraphs: "Although the *Restatement* position dominates the law, one United States Supreme Court case should be considered in the context of employee exculpation." Here again, the least effective transitional sentence is the one beginning with mechanical place-fillers, such as "The next case to be considered is" or "In addition, the court must consider." The best writing achieves fluid transition without using obvious transitional words. The best transitions are those that are not conspicuous but rather that are intrinsic to the logic and style of a particular piece of legal writing.

Simple enumeration, as in "First," "Second," "Third," or (1), (2), and (3), does more than place-filling; it provides important information to the reader. This device, often referred to as structured enumeration, is a means of identifying elements of subordinate detail and of showing how the elements relate to significant points. For example, after stating a rule of law, set out the reasons for its value: "This rule is sound for the following reasons." Either number the reasons or introduce each with "first," "second," or "third." This makes the discussion of the memorandum with others easier as well as making it easier to read.

Parallelism is another simple but useful transitional device. Two sentences each containing the same parts of speech arranged in the same order are said to be parallel, for example: "A good defense is based on more than law. A good defense is based on sound principle." Several sentences with a common subject, with or without parallel predicates, will provide smooth reading as well as reflect substantive links between ideas.

(d) Substantive Transitions Between Sentences

A substantive link serves as an excellent transition between sentences.

   1. *These holdings*, then, have to be carefully compared.

   2. Given *this historical precedent*, the court will undoubtedly affirm the judgment.

   3. If *so interpreted*, the new Act will aid our client.

4.   From *this analysis*, we may predict a similar outcome in our case.

A summary phrase referring to a subject just discussed provides transition.

1.   Plaintiff's position, *that the report is thorough and should be admitted as evidence*, is consistent with that of the government.

2.   Police officers have a proper alternative for investigating facts when, *as in this case, they suspect foul play but have no probable cause to arrest.*

3.   This holding *that federal common law should control the ownership question* was recently overruled.

4.   Just as *the actions were dissimilar in the two cases*, so also were the remedies sought.

Repetition or echo of key words or phrases serves as an effective substantive transition between sentences. Most legal terms of art function as transitions each time they are repeated. Words or phrases such as "life estate" bring to mind a complex concept that need not be restated in full each time the term is used.

The juxtaposition of two case discussions presents a common transition problem. Rather than using the citation of the second case as a crutch to move you from case to case, use substantive information. Identify (i) the similarities or differences between the cases, (ii) their chronological or jurisdictional relationships, (iii) the relative importance of the cases, or (iv) some other substantive link.

    1.   The Washington Supreme Court gives needed direction to our analysis of the facts in *Bradley* [case discussed in preceding paragraph] in its prior holding in *Arthur v. Court,* 74 Wash.2d 715, 495 P. 2d 666 (1979).

    2.   The Court in *Sisler* further expands the *Borst* decision by ruling that a child may sue the estate of a deceased parent.

    3.   The Supreme Court expanded and clarified its definition of "interrogation" in *Brewer v. Williams,* 430 U.S. 387 (1977).

(e) Transitional Words

Transitional words must be used precisely. The common transitional words "yet" and "however" are often misused; they signal a change of direction, comparable to "on the other hand." Transitional words that have several possible meanings, such as the general utility word "as," are difficult to use precisely and thus should be avoided. Transitional words with a single narrow meaning, such as "conversely," are extremely useful to the legal writer but must be used appropriately, as in the following example:

    If an employment contract does not provide for a definite period of employment, the employer may discharge the employee at any time, with or without cause. *Conversely,* an employment contract for a definite period of time is not terminable at will.

In the above example, the transitional word "conversely" capsulizes the substance of the sentence it introduces. This substantive dimension is the key to effective transitions. The best transitions are logical and substantive, not mechanical place-fillers like "and" or "in addition." They express the logical connection between what went before and what comes after.

(f) Transitions to Avoid: Nonsubstantive Place-fillers

Do not use imprecise, general transitional words or case citations to fill the place where a substantive transition should appear. Citations are attractive because they save the writer the trouble of crafting a transition and often of determining the logical connection between two sentences or paragraphs. An abbreviated case name, for example "In *Williams*," is often a false transition: it seems to move the reader from idea to idea, but it merely changes the subject.

Examples of Imprecise or Ambiguous Transitions:

1. He could not validly dispose of community property in the will *so that* part of the will is not valid.

Revised: *Because* he could not validly dispose of community property in the will, part of the will is not valid.

2. Plaintiff is factually and legally incorrect. *In addition*, Mr. Shaw was not even eligible for Social

Security benefits at the time of his death, *and* he could not qualify thereafter.

Revised: Plaintiff was factually and legally incorrect for *two reasons*. *First*, Mr. Shaw was not eligible for Social Security benefits at the time of his death. *Second*, Mr. Shaw could not qualify after his death.

3. *At the outset*, the search was made illegally because the officers had four days in which to acquire a search warrant and made no attempt to do so. (Does "at the outset" mean "to begin this argument" or "at the beginning of the event?")

Revised: The search was illegal: the officers had four days in which to acquire a search warrant and made no attempt to do so.

(g) Variety in Transitional Words

The general rule that the same word should be used to refer to the same thing should be overlooked when you are choosing transitions. If you use the word "however" or "therefore" six times in a paragraph, the reader will find it irritating, distracting, and finally meaningless. Here, and here alone, a sense of variety and elegance should prevail over consistency in word choice. The lists below are meant to provide the legal writer with alternative transitional words and phrases. Selecting a precise transition is entirely a matter of context. Each of the following transitions will work well in some contexts but not at all in others.

Common Transitional Words and Phrases

Introducing

under these circumstances	in the first place
in order to	the first reason
to a certain extent	primarily
initially, first	viewed broadly
to begin, to begin with	in general

Concluding

to conclude	therefore
to sum up, in sum	consequently
in summary	as a result
to summarize	eventually
in review	in short
to review	in brief
finally	in particular
up to this point	on the whole
thus	as we have seen

Restating

that is	in brief
to clarify	in short
in other words	in particular
in simpler terms	on the whole
to simplify	to put it differently
more simply	to be sure
to repeat	as noted

Exemplifying

for example	specifically
for instance	in particular
to illustrate	incidentally
that is	namely
as an illustration	

Emphasizing

of course	after all
to be sure	above all
indeed	actually
in fact	still
as such	especially
in effect	at least
certainly	normally
even, even so	notably
nonetheless	and rightly so
in other words	not only . . . but also

Contrasting

however	in contrast
but	nonetheless
as the same time	rather
nevertheless	in opposition to
on the contrary	opposing
contrary to	although
on the other hand	in place of
yet	conversely
and yet	actually
though	despite

alternatively	in spite of
provided that	regardless
still	instead
unlike x	notwithstanding
otherwise	even so
by contrast	even though
although this may be true	

Adding or Amplifying

again	in other words
first, second, third	equally important
once again	of equal importance
further	incidentally
furthermore	nor
moreover	analogously
too	that is
additionally	provided that
similarly	alternatively
also	in the same vein
besides	after all
beyond this	a further reason

Comparing

similarly	by analogy
in like form, manner	analogously
likewise	in the same way

Sequencing

first, second, third	in the first place
finally	last
initially	soon
next	after
then	

Cause and Effect

therefore	since
then	because
thus	for this purpose
as a result	to this end
hence	thereupon
accordingly	provided that
consequently	in effect
in consequence	

Time or Place

above	later, lately
below	initially
beyond	eventually
simultaneously	meanwhile
subsequently	since
this time	more recently
until now	adjacent to
hitherto	opposite to
elsewhere	at length
formerly	ultimately
afterwards	shortly
earlier	thereafter

Alternatives for Overworked Transitions

Therefore	*And, In addition*
then	again
thus	further
hence	furthermore
accordingly	moreover
as a result	also
consequently	too
	similarly
However, but	besides
nevertheless	likewise
on the contrary	
contrarily	
on the other hand	
yet	
still	
nonetheless	
by contrast	

CHAPTER 4

SENTENCE DESIGN

§ 4.1 INTRODUCTION

This chapter offers suggestions for writing clear sentences. After the basic principles of sentence construction are explained, several techniques for enhancing readability are described, useful sentence patterns are illustrated, and sentence structures that commonly give rise to ambiguities are pointed out.

The principles of sentence construction are few and simple. First, begin a sentence with its subject, if you can. Second, place the verb close to the subject, and place the object close to the verb. Third, place modifiers next to things they modify. Finally, end the sentence swiftly.

§ 4.2 PRINCIPLES OF SENTENCE CONSTRUCTION

(a) Begin Sentences With Significant Words or Phrases

(1) Open a Sentence With its Subject

The reader expects the subject to come first. If it does not, then the reader must remember all the words that precede the subject until the subject appears. Nonlegal professional writers place something before the subject in only 25 percent of their sentences. Legal writers do so 50 percent of the time, sometimes more often. Try to limit the number of nonsubject sentence openers that you use.

> *Example of a Confusing Nonsubject Sentence Opener*: Regarding the plaintiff's situation, it would be no clarification to state simply that Case A is or is not consistent with Case B.
>
> *Revised*: The plaintiff's situation is not clarified by stating that Case A is or is not consistent with Case B.

If you do begin a sentence with something other than its subject, use words or phrases that set the stage for the subject-verb unit to follow. Successful nonlegal professional writers limit their nonsubject sentence openers to adverbial phrases and clauses, that is, to words or phrases that establish time, place, cause, and condition.

Readers easily identify adverbial ideas as stage-setting information and easily remember such ideas until the subject appears.

(2) Place Transitional Words Near the Subject

Readers expect to find transitional words somewhere in the first part of a sentence. Such words or phrases as "on the other hand" and "in a recent Supreme Court decision" may be used to open sentences or may be placed immediately after the subject. Although transitions are important, the subject of any sentence is generally more important. Thus, many writers prefer to place transitional elements after the subject. For example, rather than opening with "On the other hand, the proponents of the second view read the statute literally," the writer may place the subject first: "The proponents of the second view, on the other hand, read the statute literally." This places initial emphasis on the subject, "proponents," and final emphasis on the way in which the proponents read the statute, "literally."

(3) Do Not Routinely Open Sentences With Full Citations

Avoid the habitual use of a full citation as a sentence opener. The writer should spare the reader from having to comprehend or skip over a full citation in order to arrive at the point of a sentence.   Whenever possible, place a full citation at the end of a sentence, preferably in a separate citation sentence, as demonstrated below.

> *Awkward opening*: In *Kosters v. Seven-Up Co.*, 595 F.2d 347 (6th Cir. 1979), the court held that a franchiser was liable for breach of warranty to an ultimate consumer who was injured by a defective product.

> *Revised*: A franchiser has been held liable for breach of warranty to an ultimate consumer who was injured by a defective product. *Kosters v. Seven-Up Co.*, 595 F.2d 347 (6th Cir. 1979).

The separate sentence citation is permissible if the cited authority supports or contradicts the full statement in the preceding sentence. If the cited authority supports or contradicts only part of the statement in the sentence, the citation must follow that part of the sentence.

> A franchiser has been held liable to an ultimate consumer for breach of warranty, *Kosters v. Seven-Up Co.*, 595 F.2d 347 (6th Cir. 1979), but a licensor of personal property has been held not liable on warranty grounds, *Shaw v. Fairyland at Harvey's Inc.*, 26 App.Div.2d 576, 271 N.Y.S.2d 70 (1966).

If the writer wishes to emphasize a case name or other authority for which the citation has not yet been given, then the case citation may begin the sentence. For example, *"Buckley v. Valeo*, 424 U.S. 1 (1976), is the leading case on federal regulation of campaign spending." Even where a case is being emphasized, however, the complete citation may be placed last to improve readability: "The leading case on federal regulation of campaign spending is *Buckley v. Valeo*, 424 U. S. 1 (1976)."

When deciding whether to place a full citation first or last, ask yourself if the reader will need that information before reading the subject-verb unit. If not, then the citation will be a visual obstacle for the reader.

Shortened citation forms do not create such an obstacle, for example, " 'Outrageous conduct,' 316 U.S. at 7, was the court's characterization of the law officer's treatment of the defendant." Shortened names of cases or other authorities may serve as helpful transitional elements. The shortened citation or case name may be placed first in the sentence, or it may be placed after the subject as follows:

> The Court in *Buckley* circumscribes federal regulation of campaign spending.

(b) Keep Subject and Verb Close Together

Subject and verb should be kept as close together as possible. As English speakers, we understand the subject and verb only as a unit, that is, neither subject nor verb is fully processed until the other is discovered. Keep verbs and objects close together for the same reason.

If a subject and verb (or a verb and object) must be separated, then they should be separated by no more than ten words. This seemingly arbitrary rule requires an explanation. Our short-term memory accurately holds seven items, for example, telephone numbers, physical objects such as cars or pedestrians in an intersection, decimal digits, and monosyllabic words. (This mnemonic limit is sometimes referred to as the Magical Number Seven, Plus or Minus Two.) Thus, for each group of seven words in a sentence, there must be what is called "closure"; that is, the words must form a self-enclosed unit, for example (i) a subject with modifiers ("the case on appeal"), (ii) phrases ("in other words"), and (iii) clauses ("that the court will recognize").

We read and remember in segments. Social security numbers and telephone numbers are segmented to help us remember them. In the same way, sentences must be segmented (have frequent closure) if the reader is to understand on first reading. In reality, lawyers and law students are compelled to read sentences containing segments of a dozen words or more. Each word in such a segment must be held individually in the short-term memory until the segment is closed. If closure is delayed too long, the reader forgets the initial words in the segment and so must reread.

Perhaps because lawyers have daily practice with long segments of words, they appear to have an ability to hold more than seven items in the short-term memory (or at least they tolerate the strain). The legal writer may thus wish to observe the Magical Number limit when writing for lay readers and to extend it slightly when writing for legally trained readers. Ten words is a reasonable limit for the legal writer to observe when writing for other lawyers. Longer gaps are not "wrong," of course; they simply compel the reader to reread the sentence.

Subject and Verb Too Far Apart: *Continuation* [S] of partnership upon retirement, death, or bankruptcy of a partner and *disposition of* [S_2] the partnership interests of the retiring, deceased, or bankrupt partner *should be* [V] subject to majority vote.

Revision that Keeps Subject and Verb Together: *Continuation* [S_1] of partnership *should be* [V_1] subject to majority vote after any partner retires, dies, or suffers bankruptcy. At that time, *disposition of partnership interests* [S_2] *should* also *be* [V_2] subject to majority vote.

Subject and Verb may be moved closer together in various ways, as in these two additional revisions of the first sentence:

1. If a partner retires, dies, or suffers bankruptcy, *continuation* [S_1] of partnership *should be* [V_1] subject to majority vote.

2. After the retirement, death, or bankruptcy of a partner, *continuation* [S_1] of partnership *should be* [V_1] subject to majority vote.

(c) Use Subject-Verb-Object Pattern

Nearly all sentences should be written in the active voice, that is, following the Subject-Verb-Object pattern. This is the pattern most readily comprehended by English speakers. When the doer of an action is in the Subject position (and the receiver of an action is in the Object position), the sentence is active and thus most forceful: "Defendant's car hit the plaintiff's fence." When the doer of an action is moved to the Object position and the receiver of an action is moved to the Subject position (that is, Subject and Object are reversed), the sentence is passive and tends to lose forcefulness. "The plaintiff's fence was hit by the defendant's car."

When deciding whether to use active or passive voice, ask yourself, first, whether the reader needs to know the subject and, second, whether you want the reader to know the subject. If the answer to either question is affirmative, then use the active voice. If the answer is negative, use the passive.

The passive voice is useful if you wish to:

(i) emphasize what was done rather than who did it:

The defendant's car was crushed.

(ii) vary sentence structure:

The clerk reviewed the record. The judge studied the record and the briefs. Afterward they agreed that *the record had been misread by* both counsel.

(iii) depersonalize tone by making acts anonymous:

The records were misplaced.

(iv) emphasize facts:

Drawers had been pulled out, clothes were strewn about the floor, even valuable jewelry had been scattered over the dresser top. These facts, found by the lower court, emphasize the reckless nature of the sheriff's search.

The passive voice is also useful if you do not know the subject or wish to deny responsibility.

During the investigation, it was noted that the recording equipment had been tampered with. (name or rank or position of investigator unknown or best left unsaid)

(d) Keep Related Parts of the Sentence Together

(1) Introduction

The most common result of not keeping related words together is the misplaced modifier. A misplaced modifier is a word, phrase, or clause that appears to modify the wrong thing. Modifiers should be placed next to the word or words that they modify. Misplaced modifiers can occur at any point in a sentence and often result in ambiguity.

Keep this general rule in mind: If a reader must reread a sentence in order to determine what modifies what, then the sentence is poorly constructed and should be rewritten. A charitable reader will be able to sort out most ambiguous modifiers. The legal writer cannot, however, rely on the charity of legal readers. If any two lawyers are asked the meaning of a sentence with an ambiguous modifier, they may give the same interpretation if they consider the sentence in the abstract. Their answers may differ, however, if they must consider the sentence from the viewpoints of clients with conflicting interests.

In a recent case, for example, a $55,000 judgment rested on the interpretation of an allegedly misplaced word. The disputed word, which cost the losing side the full $55,000, was "available": "The scour protection fill may be pit-run gravel available in natural position on shore at the project site or other suitable material acceptable to the engineer." The question was whether the fill "may be available" or whether pit-run gravel is available and may be used as fill. Depending on the drafter's intent, the sentence should have been written either of two ways:

> The fill may or may not be available in natural position.

The pit-run gravel that is available may be used as fill.

(2) Avoid Misplaced Modifiers at the Beginning of a Sentence

1. *Confusing*: By doing so, the security interest will not survive bankruptcy. (Who is "doing so"? Not the "security interest.")

Clear: If we do so, the security interest will not survive bankruptcy.

2. *Confusing*: As your lawyer, the dog must be leashed.

Clear: As your lawyer, I advise you to leash your dog.

(3) Avoid Misplaced Modifiers in the Middle of a Sentence

Modifying words or phrases may "squint," that is, look both ways, in the middle of a sentence. Adverbs like "well," "only," "often," and "both" are particularly troublesome in mid-sentence.

1. A lawyer who can write *well* deserves her fee. (Does any lawyer who can write deserve her fee? Or do only those who write *well* deserve it?)

Revised by rephrasing: A lawyer who is a skilled writer deserves her fee.

2. A contractor who fails to complete construction on time often cannot be made to pay a penalty. (If a contractor fails often, then he cannot be made to pay? Or is it often the case that contractors who fail to complete construction on time cannot be made to pay?)

Revise by moving "often" or by substituting "cannot always be made to pay."

3.   The decision favors *both* the positions taken in *Copra* and *Coldewey*. (Both positions taken in each case? One position taken in both cases? Two distinct positions, one in each case? More than one position taken in each case?)

Revise by writing out in full.

(4) Avoid Split Infinitives

Infinitives should be split only if ambiguity or awkwardness results from leaving them intact.

Writers sometimes place modifiers inside an infinitive ("to *unduly* influence," "to *specifically* perform") to avoid such ambiguous sentences as these:

The court imposed new requirements *strictly to regulate* interstate sales of toxic sprays.

The court imposed new requirements *to regulate strictly* interstate sales of toxic sprays.

If the adverb "strictly" is not to modify either "imposed" (meaning "imposed in a strict way") or "interstate" (meaning "exclusively interstate"), then the infinitive "to regulate" must be split:

The court imposed new requirements *to strictly regulate* interstate sales of toxic sprays.

Sentences that require a split infinitive, like the above example, are relatively few. A simple revision will usually eliminate the potential ambiguity without the need for splitting the infinitive.

Unnecessarily Split Infinitive: Judicial discretion allows the court *to both fulfill* its role as parens patriae to the child and *to fully consider* the right of the child.

Revised: Judicial discretion allows the court *both to fulfill* its role as parens patriae to the child and *to consider fully* the rights of the child.

(5) Avoid Ambiguous Modifiers at the End of a Sentence

Avoid unwanted ambiguity stemming from ambiguous modifiers at the end.

1. *Confusing*: The court reviewed the 1965 Act in its dicta, changing the requirements for good faith bargaining. (Dicta changes? The Act changes? The Court changes?)

Clear: In its dicta, the Court reviewed the 1965 Act, which changes the requirements for good faith bargaining. (The Act changes.)

2. *Confusing*: "Affiliate of the Partnership of the General Partners" does not include a Person who is a Partner in a partnership with the Partnership or with the General Partners or their affiliates, *which person* is not otherwise an Affiliate of the Partnership of the General Partners. (Which person?)

(e) End Sentences Swiftly and Effectively

As soon as you have completed a subject-verb unit, consider ending the sentence. Continue to write another subject-verb unit in the same sentence only if ideas are so closely related that they must be joined.

(1) Put Significant Words or Phrases in the Final Position

The two "emphatic positions" in a sentence are the beginning and the end. Be certain that the words you place in these two emphatic positions deserve to be there.

Unemphatic: We recommend that the Company discuss with us further its plans for obtaining outside investment *in the future*.

Revised: We recommend that the Company discuss with us further its plans for obtaining future *outside investment*.

(2) Avoid Prepositional Phrases in the Final Position

Final prepositional phrases are usually weak and sometimes ambiguous.

Rhetorically Weak and Ambiguous Series of Prepositions: Also enclosed is a letter I prepared *in* response *to* a request *for* explanation *of* certain features *of* an individual employment contract *for* a plant superintendent.

Revised: Also enclosed is a letter I prepared for a plant superintendent to explain certain features of an individual employment contract.

Or: Also enclosed is a letter I prepared to explain certain features of a plant superintendent's individual employment contract.

§ 4.3   TECHNIQUES TO ENHANCE READABILITY

(a) Use Short and Medium-Length Sentences

The best professional prose on complex or technical subjects averages 20 words per sentence. For legal writers, this average is slightly higher (20 to 25 words per sentence). Although a variety of sentence lengths is important for avoiding monotony (which actually retards comprehension), even the longer sentences normally should not exceed 35 words.

To determine your average number of words per sentence, take a representative sample of your prose (at least 250 words) and count the words. Count as single words hyphenated words, abbreviations, numbers, and case names. Omit citation sentences from the count. In citations within a sentence, consider as single words the case name, the reported citation, and the date. Next count the number of sentences and divide for the average. If it is greater than 25, you should concentrate on writing shorter sentences. Using the same writing sample, check for variety in sentence lengths: sentences should vary from short to long without monotony in length or pattern of occurrence. There should be some short, some medium, and some long, but not in any discernible order.

(b) Make One Point Per Sentence

Two related ideas may be joined by a semicolon without significantly lessening readability. In general, however, keep separate thoughts in separate sentences.

(c) Make Sentences Affirmative, Not Negative

We understand affirmative statements more quickly and easily than negative ones. In studies of the effects of language on the mind, researchers have found that affirmative statements are psychologically more linear than negative ones: with negatives we must first understand the affirmative sense, then negate it. This is analogous to understanding another language by first translating it into one's own. Avoid these nearly incomprehensible combinations: "not otherwise," "never unless," "none unless," "never otherwise," and so forth.

Negative Sentence: The Plaintiff must not be prevented from bringing suit to a court because of the binding power of an arbitration clause that is merely part of a larger contract.

Affirmative Revision: The Plaintiff must be allowed to bring a suit to a court regardless of the binding power of an arbitration clause that is merely part of a larger contract.

Confusing Negative Words or Ideas:

1. Contrary to opposing counsel's denial, the facts dispose of the primary defense.

Revised: The facts contradict the primary defense raised by counsel for the defendant.

2. Not only is there no evidence that Mr. Jones relied upon the booklet, but also, even if he had, it would not change the outcome of this case.

Revised: Even if Mr. Jones had relied upon the booklet (and evidence is lacking), the outcome would remain the same.

(d) Use Parallelism and Balance in Sentence Structures

Parallelism is similarity of structure, that is, repetition of like words in the same order, for example, "He came, he saw, he conquered." A reader will be better able to absorb new information if parallel structures are used because the structure will be "transparent." That is, only the meaning of the words themselves must be processed, not a new structure. Compare this nonparallel structure with the above version: "After he came, he looked and then conquered."

Parallel structure is particularly helpful in a sentence containing multiple subjects, verbs, or objects. Legal writers frequently use such compound structures, which tend to be confusing unless they are given parallel structure. If a compound structure must be used, keep word order and parts of speech the same when possible, for example, "We agreed *to trade photographs* and not *to exchange bills.*"

Balanced structure refers to groupings of words which are of roughly the same length. Such structures need not be worded similarly. They need only "sound" rhythmical to the reader's ear. Rhythmic patterns within sentences, as well as a rhythmic variation of sentences within paragraphs, increase readability in two ways. First, rhythmic patterns allow the reader's mind to anticipate how much attention will be required for each syllable to come. This makes reading easier. In the same way, music in which sound patterns are rhythmic is easier to listen to than music in which every note comes as a surprise. When there is a discernible melody, we can prepare for what is to come; thus we process what *does* come more quickly.

Effective use of parallelism and balance also lends emphasis and allows density (greater detail) without loss of readability.

Effective Use of Parallelism and Balance:

The conduct of the officers in *searching Mr. Smiley, seizing his property,* and *arresting him* is exactly the type of conduct the fourth amendment was designed to prevent.

Revision for Parallelism:

Without Parallelism: The Company should place on its stock certificates a disclaimer and should make a notation in its stock records.

Revised: The Company should place a disclaimer on its stock certificates and make a notation on its stock records.

(e) Provide Extra Structural Clues

(1) Include Essential "That"

Although it sometimes may properly be omitted, the word "that" is frequently essential to correct reading of a sentence. It is not an "extra" clue in these instances but rather an essential structural clue. The italicized phrases or clauses in the following examples may be misread as discrete units. Without the essential structural clue, the reader may have to reread these sentences for initial comprehension.

1. The complainant has the burden of *proving the rates* violate the statute. (The reader wonders initially how the complainant will "prove rates.")

Revised: The complainant has the burden of proving *that* the rates violate the statute.

2. When a manufacturer advertises his product, *he knows his acts* may have consequences in another state and that he may be held liable. (The reader finds initially that a manufacturer "knows his acts," a comforting, if obvious, idea.)

[*81*]

Revised: When a manufacturer advertises his products, he knows *that* his acts may have consequences in another state and that he may be held liable.

(2) Repeat Some Structure Words to Improve Readability

1. I am aware that the securities are not being registered under the federal Securities Act of 1933 or any state securities laws, pursuant to exemptions from registration.

Revised: I am aware that the securities are not being registered under the federal Securities Act of 1933 or *under* any state securities laws, pursuant to exemptions from registration.

2. We recommend that the Company discuss with us its plans for obtaining future outside investment and granting stock options.

Revised: We recommend that the Company discuss with us its plans for obtaining future outside investment and *for* granting stock options.

§ 4.4 USEFUL SENTENCE PATTERNS FOR LEGAL WRITING

(a) Basic Sentence Types

Of the three basic sentence types (simple, compound, and complex), simple and complex should dominate legal writing.

Most sentences should be simple in structure, that is, one subject-verb unit. Use an occasional four-to-six word sentence for emphasis. The simple sentence is the pattern best suited for expressing one idea at a time—something all legal writers should attempt to do.

> *Simple*: Subject (*S*) + Verb (*V*)
> (The boat   leaks.)

If two ideas must be included in the same sentence, the complex sentence pattern may be more economical than the compound.

> *Complex*:
>
> (i) *S* + *V*, Subordinating Conjunction *S* + *V*
> (The boat did not sink, even though it leaks.)
>
> (ii) Subordinating Conjunction + *S* + *V*, *S* + *V*
> (Even though the boat leaks, it did not sink.)

Subordinating conjunctions include:

after	inasmuch as	until
although	in order that	when
as	in that	whenever
as if	provided	where
because	since	wherever
before	so that	whether
how	that	while
if	unless	

> *Compound*:
>
> (i) *S* + *V*, Coordinating Conjunction *S* + *V*
> (The boat did not sink, but it leaks.)
>
> (ii)   *S* + *V*; *S* + *V*.
> (The boat leaks; it did not sink.)

Coordinating conjunctions include:

and	for	or
but	nor	yet

(iii) $S + V$; Conjunctive Adverb, $S + V$
(The boat leaks; however, it did not sink.)

(iv) S, Conjunctive Adverb, V; $S + V$
(The boat, however, did not sink; it simply leaks.).

Conjunctive adverbs include:

also	in fine	so
as a result	likewise	still
besides	moreover	therefore
consequently	nevertheless	thus
henceforth	notwithstanding	yet
however	otherwise	

The complex pattern is more efficient than the compound because it establishes a logical and a hierarchical relationship between two ideas. Because a subordinating conjunction subordinates one subject-verb unit to another, the relative importance of the two ideas in a complex sentence is automatically reflected by the sentence structure. Compare the relative importance of the two ideas (subject-verb units) in the following sentences:

1. *Compound Sentence Pattern*: The construction costs have exceeded the original amounts by 55%, and Mr. Baggins is unable to settle this case.

Complex Sentence Pattern: Because the construction costs have exceeded the original amounts by 55%, Mr. Baggins is unable to settle this case.

In the complex sentence, emphasis falls on Mr. Baggins' inability to settle the case. In the compound sentence, the uninformative word "and" does nothing more than establish a loose connection, rather like a "plus" in addition. It carries no other information about the relationship between the clauses it joins.

2. *Compound*: The wage differential has existed since the initial hiring of the coaches, so it would be very difficult for the school district to assert seniority as the basis for that differential.

Complex: Inasmuch as the wage differential has existed since the initial hiring of the coaches, it would be very difficult for the school district to assert seniority as the basis for that differential.

(b) Useful Patterns: "If . . . Then"

An "If . . . then" sentence pattern may be used to establish a condition, to describe a complex cause-and-effect situation, or to detail a sequence of events. This pattern permits complexity without a wide separation of subject and verb. Both the "if-clause" and the "then-clause" contain their own subject-verb units, making them easier for the reader to grasp. A "When . . . then" structure works identically, but has a slightly different meaning. The word "then"

[*85*]

need not be included in the sentence, although it does assist the reader.

Ordinarily, use no more than two "if-clauses" in a sentence. A succession of "if-clauses" leading to a final "then-clause" will be hard to comprehend on one reading. You should indent and enumerate if more than two "if-clauses" are needed before a "then-clause" can follow.

1. *Confusing*: We will not discuss a settlement with you without the *manager prevailing* upon her bookkeeper to compile a final statement covering all construction costs and *allowing* Sam Perkins to look at the books and records and satisfy himself that things were done properly.

Revised: *If the manager* will prevail upon her bookkeeper to compile a final statement covering all construction costs and *if the manager* will allow Sam Perkins to look at the books and records and satisfy himself that things were done properly, *then* we will discuss a settlement.

2. *Confusing*: We ask *that this be done* and *that the management problem be openly and honestly discussed* in order that the matter be settled amicably and at the least possible expense to both parties.

Revised: *If the management* problem is discussed openly and honestly, *then* the matter can be settled amicably and at the least possible expense.

In the first example, the second modifier "allowing" is too far from the noun it modifies ("manager") for rapid comprehension. The reader must reread the sentence. An "if . . .

then" structure eliminates this problem. In the second example, the double object and the lengthy clause beginning "in order that" extend the sentence beyond the length comfortable for most readers.

(c) Useful Patterns: Stating a Rule and Exception

If a rule and an exception occur in the same sentence, the rule should be stated first. The reader will not understand the exception fully or remember it well without the rule already in mind. The best way to handle rules, exceptions, and conditions is to give each its own sentence, for example, "As a general rule . . .. An exception, however, is . . .."

> The court has consistently recognized an absolute immunity for statements made in judicial proceedings. If a person has suffered special injury in such proceedings, however, the court has recognized an exception to that immunity by approving an action for malicious prosecution.

(d) Useful Patterns: Reversal of Direct Object and Prepositional Phrases

When the direct object is longer and more detailed than a prepositional phrase that modifies the verb, the prepositional phrase may be placed first after the verb. This gives the reader a better chance of remembering the verb while reading both the direct object and the prepositional phrase.

Confusing: Cynthia Williams of Browning Associates *transferred* [*V*] the *property* [*DO*] that had been held in trust for twenty-five years *to George Berry* [*PP*].

Clear: Cynthia Williams of Browning Associates *transferred* [*V*] *to George Berry* [*PP*] the *property* [*DO*] that had been held in trust for twenty-five years.

(e) Useful Patterns: Periodic Sentence

In the periodic sentence, the main thought is not completed until the end of the sentence, thus creating suspense and taking full advantage of the final emphatic position.

1. If the individual arrested is diagnosed as an alcoholic, early commitment for effective treatment, either on a voluntary or involuntary basis, is essential.

2. When you consider the chaos that ensued, it is remarkable that anyone—witnesses, victims, or defendant—can recall the details of the automobile collision.

To achieve its effect, the periodic sentence is often opened with "it" or "there" or "the fact that." These pronouns or other "place-fillers" stand in for the subject (itself reserved for a later or final position in the sentence). Although this sentence pattern can be effective if used sparingly, it is sometimes overused in legal writing, especially in argument. Use it with care and only for special emphasis.

§ 4.5 PRINCIPLES FOR AVOIDING AMBIGUOUS OR CONFUSING SENTENCES

(a) Avoid the "Not . . . Because" Sentence Pattern

If the word "not" comes before the word "because" in a sentence, the sentence may be ambiguous. It will frequently be hard to read, whether or not it is ambiguous. The reader may not know whether you mean "Not because of this, but rather because of that" or whether you mean "Not so, and for this reason."

1. *Confusing*: The fact that no mention of Defendant was made in the will does not preclude her because she is his legal heir. (Because she is his heir, lack of mention will not preclude her? Or does it preclude her not because she is his heir but rather because of something else?)

Clear: Because she is his legal heir, the absence of a mention of her in the will does not preclude her.

2. *Confusing*: The threshold requirement of a common core of tasks is not met because of the inherent differences between coaching baseball and coaching tennis. (Requirement is not met because of differences but rather because of something else? Or differences prevent the requirement from being met?)

Clear: Because there are inherent differences between coaching baseball and coaching tennis, the threshold requirement of a common core of tasks is not met.

(b) Avoid Ambiguous Prepositional Phrases

(1) Introduction

Prepositional phrases present many challenges to the legal writer. They are easily misplaced and thus often misread. Ambiguities frequently result from strings of prepositional phrases inside a sentence and from prepositional phrases beginning with the word "with" at the end of a sentence.

(2) Place Prepositional Phrases Next to What They Modify

Ambiguous: Plaintiff pleads that the letter was found to be insufficient in Paragraph IV of his complaint. (In Paragraph IV, the letter was insufficient?)

Precise: Plaintiff pleads, in Paragraph IV of his complaint, that the letter was found to be insufficient.

(3) Avoid Strings of Prepositional Phrases

Multiple prepositional phrases may be ambiguous, especially at the end of a sentence. The following sentence, for example, may be read to mean a number of things, including the anarchical idea that justice is based on the individual's capacity for self-government.

The continued existence of a free and democratic society depends *upon recognition of the concept* that justice is based *upon the rule of law* grounded *in respect for the dignity of the individual* and his capacity *through reason for enlightened self-government.*

(4) Beware of Adjacent Prepositional Phrases

Ambiguous: They examined every figure in the account in defendant's handwriting. (Is the entire account in defendant's handwriting or just some of the figures?)

Precise: They examined every figure that defendant had written in the account.

(5) Beware of "With" and "Without" Phrases in Final Position

These phrases are sometimes ambiguous at the end of a sentence. Substitute more precise words.

Ambiguous structure: Noun + Verb + Object + *with* + Noun

1. *Ambiguous*: Our client will finance the contract with expenses. (Client will finance with expenses?)

Precise: Our client will finance the contract and the expenses.

2. *Ambiguous*: Several courts have found jurisdiction proper for a private complainant without any interpretation of the statute.

Precise: Without interpreting the statute, several courts have found jurisdiction proper for a private complainant.

(c) Avoid Sentences Beginning With Relative Pronouns

Sentences beginning with "who," "which," or "that" will probably require rereading unless they are short.

1.   *That* the group associated for the sole purpose of committing crimes constitutes a pattern of racketeering activity.

Revised: A pattern of racketeering is established because the group associated for the sole purpose of committing crimes.

2.   *Which* decision the court will uphold is, given the balance of authority, impossible accurately to predict.

Revised: Because the decisions are of equal weight, it is impossible to predict which the court will uphold.

3.   *Whom* the opposing counsel uses as expert witnesses will determine the cross-examination strategy we will adopt.

Revised: Our cross-examination strategy will depend on whom opposing counsel uses as expert witnesses.

§ 4.6 SENTENCE REVISION

(a) A Simple Method for Revising Troublesome Sentences

(1) First, Lift Main Subject, Verb, and Object From the Sentence

Reread each unsatisfactory sentence quickly to find the subject, verb, and object, and "lift" them from the rest of the sentence. The following sentence, for example, needs revision:

> Having determined, as it has, that the protection of the public's interest in the shorelines, in water quality, in air quality, and in other subjects, requires compliance with a carefully drawn statutory scheme, the legislature is not entitled to single out one specific activity or category of project for exception from the scheme in that its motive is clearly to sacrifice environmental protection to speeding up the licensing process.

Main Subject: "legislature"

Main Verb Phrase: "is not entitled to single out"

Objects: "one activity," "category"

If the key idea is "legislature is not entitled to single out one activity or category," then the revision should begin with that key idea. The idea should not be buried in the middle of the sentence, but should instead appear in a separate sentence.

Revised: The legislature is not entitled to single out one activity or category for exception from the statutory scheme. (The rest of the example is revised below.)

(2) Second, Remove Imprecise Subject-Verb Combinations

Fuzzy sentences are often the result of an imprecise subject-verb combination. This imprecision, hidden by the rest of the sentence, becomes evident when the subject and verb are lifted from the rest of the sentence.

> *Initial subject and verb from above example*: [T]he *protection* . . . *requires* compliance.

This fuzzy notion, that "protection" can somehow "require" something, obscures the thought in the sentence. The subject, or the "who" in the sentence, should be the legislature: "the legislature requires compliance in order to protect the public's interest."

(3) Third, Revise for Subject-Verb-Object Order

After you have isolated the subject and verb, consider moving the subject to the beginning of the sentence. This often means relocating an initial phrase or clause, such as the clause in (1) above: "Having determined, as it has, that the protection of the public's interest in the shorelines, in water quality, in air quality, and in other subjects, requires compliance with a carefully drawn statutory scheme." This 33-word introductory clause should be converted to a sentence of its own, again by first locating the subject(s) and verb(s) and then by revising:

Legislature [S] has determined [V] (that) protection [S₂] requires [V₂] compliance [O₂].

Revised: The legislature has determined that compliance with a carefully drawn statutory scheme is required for protection of the public's interest in the shorelines, in water quality, in air quality, and in other subjects.

Thus, the original long sentence has been revised by several simple procedures, into three shorter sentences:

Revised: The legislature has determined that compliance with a carefully drawn statutory scheme is required for protection of the public's interest in the shorelines, in water quality, in air quality, and in other subjects. Having done so, the legislature is not entitled to single out one activity or category for exception from the statutory scheme. The legislature's motive for making such exceptions is to speed up the licensing process at the expense of environmental protection.

(b) Simple Techniques for Shortening Sentences

(1) Introduction

Long sentences may be broken into several shorter ones as demonstrated below by (i) eliminating unnecessary words, (ii) converting long sentences to simpler, shorter ones, and (iii) transferring parenthetical expressions to another sentence.

(2) Eliminate Unnecessary Words

The legal writer must learn to distinguish between redundancy and helpful repetition of words or ideas. Do not, for example, eliminate structural clues, as described in a preceding section. Do, however, eliminate such redundancies as "basic fundamentals" or "with lucid clarity."

If time permits, reread each word and ask yourself, "Do I need this word? Will anything significant be lost if I take it out?" If you do this, you will begin to form the habit of writing concisely. Occasionally, words that could be left out improve the rhythm of a sentence or paragraph. Improved sound or rhythm is, however, no excuse for using flabby intensifiers like "very" and "pretty much." When excess is removed, emphasis occurs naturally and rhythm is improved.

Avoid writing sentences beginning with an unnecessary "It . . . that" structure.

   1. *Wordy*: It is the theory that lends itself . . .

Concise: The theory lends itself . . .

   2. *Wordy*: It must be noted, however, that the authority . . .

Concise: Note, however, that the authority . . .

3. *Wordy*: It can be said with certainty, moreover, that a structural violation will be recognized by all courts.

Concise: Moreover, a structural violation will certainly be recognized by all courts.

4. *Wordy*: Again, it should be emphasized that it is doubtful that a naked allegation of mismanagement of funds by the trustees would confer jurisdiction.

Concise: A naked allegation of mismanagement of funds by the trustees would probably not confer jurisdiction.

5. *Wordy*: It is unlikely that one who fails to make a case of wage discrimination under the Equal Pay Act would prevail with the same claim under Title VII.

Concise: One who fails to make a case of wage discrimination under the Equal Pay Act is not likely to prevail with the same claim under Title VII.

Also avoid sentences beginning with an "In that the" structure, and avoid internal clauses beginning with "in that." These are clumsy, difficult to read, and verbose.

Wordy: In that the witness is also an interested party, his testimony is suspect.

Concise: The witness's testimony is suspect because he is an interested party.

Or: Because he is an interested party, the witness's testimony is suspect.

(3) Avoid Stating the Obvious

Obvious: If Dr. West had recognized Peter's dangerousness and had warned Paul, Peter would have been deterred from killing Paul—an act which had unpleasant consequences for both boys.

(4) Convert Long Compound Sentences to Shorter Sentences

Replace "and," "but," "or," "nor," and "for" with a period.

If he was not insured on reaching the age of 65, he does not become insured by reason of any insurable employment which he takes up later, and the special contributions which are payable under the Act by his employer only, in respect of such employment, do not give him any title to health insurance benefits or pension, and moreover a man is not at liberty to pay any contributions on his own account as a voluntary contributor for any period after his 65th birthday.

Revised: If he was not insured at age 65, he does not become insured by reason of any insurable employment that he takes up later. The special contributions that are payable under the Act by his employer only, in respect of such employment, do not give him any title to health insurance benefits or pension. Moreover, a man is not at liberty to pay any contributions on his own account as a voluntary contributor for any period after his 65th birthday.

(5) Transfer Parenthetical Expressions to Another Sentence

Too Long: The district court in Maryland in a recent case stated that the EEOC's policy of sending right-to-use letters immediately after the filing of the charge, *if the regional director ascertains that the charge cannot be investigated within 180 days*, was "inconsistent with an obvious congressional intent."

Revised: The EEOC's policy is to send right-to-sue letters immediately after the filing of the charge, *if the regional director ascertains that the charge cannot be investigated within 180 days*. The district court in a recent case stated that the policy was "inconsistent with an obvious congressional intent."

(c) How to Acquire Efficient Revision Habits

Few legal writers have time to revise every sentence they write. Fewer still have time to follow each of the above suggestions every time they write. How can a legal writer, writing every day under pressure, acquire good revision habits?

The answer is to acquire them slowly, one by one. Take one suggestion for revision at a time, for example: "Use short sentences." Review the next piece you write for sentence length. Read each sentence, and shorten those that are too long. This may take an extra few minutes, but it will "program" your "mental computer" to be alert for overlong sentences. Repeat this for the next few pieces of writing. The human brain is a miraculous machine; it will absorb your new revision technique and incorporate it into your intuitive writing style.

Then select another tip for revision. For example, review for sentence openers. Revise so that most sentences open with their subjects. Repeat this for the next few pieces of writing. If your "computer" was well programmed for sentence length, then you will automatically be checking for that as well. A few days or weeks later, select a third strategy, for example, subject-verb distance. Review each sentence for that. Continue with this system until you have "programmed" a solution to each of the writing problems you have. This "programming" will require a small investment of time at first but will ultimately save time, both for you and for your readers.

Those revision practices that you select—those that suit your personal style—will become part of your intuitive editorial behavior, both while writing and afterwards during revision. Once they become part of your intuitive writing behavior, you will write faster and more effectively.

CHAPTER 5

LANGUAGE IN THE LEGAL SETTING

The most important matter is to identify the ideas
. . . but the choice of the word to express the idea
is of almost equal importance. The expressions of
one whose ideas are confused and uncertain will of
necessity be equally confusing to others; but the effort to choose a word that will clearly convey an idea
to others is of great assistance in clarifying to oneself the idea that should be conveyed.

—3 *Corbin on Contracts* 7 (1960)

§ 5.1 INTRODUCTION

Correct usage of legal and nonlegal language
is fundamental to clear writing, but in a given
context there is seldom only one "correct" word
choice. The introduction to language in this
chapter is intended to help the legal writer make
effective choices as well as correct choices. The
introduction includes principles for word selection
and a discussion of redundancy in legal writing.
The chapter concludes with a glossary of words
commonly misused in legal writing.

[*101*]

§ 5.2 PRINCIPLES FOR MAKING WORD CHOICES

To say precisely what we mean requires thought: first, we must identify what we mean, and, second, we must decide how best to express it. Many writers use the words that come automatically to mind, however, without giving them further thought. These automatic word choices are not necessarily the best choices. The following principles will help you to make effective word choices rather than automatic word choices.

(a) Use Words in Their Literal Sense

Two common sources of imprecision in legal writing are personification (the giving of human qualities to abstractions or objects, for example, "cold-blooded decision") and metonymy (the substitution of an attributive or a suggestive word for the word identifying a person or thing, for example, "stage hand" for "stage worker"). In some writings, this kind of imprecision may be acceptable; in legal writing, it may introduce ambiguity.

1. *Imprecise*: California has so held.

Precise: The California Court of Appeals has so held.

2. *Imprecise*: This Washington case so found.

Precise: The jury in this Washington case so found.

3. *Imprecise*: The five points analyze the statute.

Precise: The court analyzes the statute in five points.

(b) Omit Archaic Legalisms

"Archaic legalisms" are words and phrases, such as "hereinafter," "heretofore," "aforesaid," "forthwith," "herein," "hereby," "for purposes hereof," "notwithstanding anything to the contrary herein," "so made," "by these presents," and "said." Not only are these words obstacles to the lay reader, but they are also imprecise and thus troublesome to the legal reader. For example, the words "thereof" and "therefrom" can be removed from the following sentence without loss of meaning:

> The following assets for administration under this Article 4, including the proceeds, investments and reinvestments thereof, and accumulated income therefrom, if any, shall constitute the "trust estate."

The more serious fault of archaic legalisms is that they may create the appearance of precision, thus obscuring ambiguities that might otherwise be recognized. For example, a question that has been frequently litigated is whether "herein" refers to the paragraph in which it is used, to the section, or to the whole document. Therefore, after removing the archaic language, consider whether you must add precise references to time, place, or concept.

(c) Use the Same Word to Refer to the Same Thing; Use Different Words to Refer to Different Things

Never attempt to improve style by introducing synonyms or other word variations that will create confusion or ambiguity. In the following sentences, the substitution of the word "prevailing" for the word "dominant" creates initial confusion: Is the author going to discuss two views?

> According to the *dominant view*, this article is applied to periodic meetings as well as to special meetings. The *prevailing view* is that Article 237 of the Commercial Code provides the right for minority shareholders to convene either type of meeting.

Similarly, from the following sentence can we know whether the author is discussing two or three forms of copyright?

> Although under the old Act a *common law copyright* existed in writings until they qualified for statutory protection, the *non-statutory copyright* was extinguished when the *statutory copyright* was created by publication or registration.

A corollary is to use different words when you mean different things. If the same word is used to mean different things, the reader will be at least momentarily confused.

> 1. In *case* of litigation in the present *case*, the accountant's testimony will be crucial.

2. In a sub*point* to the second argument, the court makes the *point* that intent should control.

3. As a final *consideration*, there was no discussion of the contractor's *consideration*.

4. Under our present system of criminal *sanctions*, legislative limits and judicial discretion *sanction* substantial sentence individualization.

(d) Use Simple, Familiar Words

When you have a choice between a short, familiar word, such as "call," and a longer, more elaborate word, such as "communicate," choose the shorter, simpler one. Simple words are understood more quickly; they require less reading and thinking time.

Simple Words	*Elaborate Counterparts*
after	subsequent to
before	prior to
begin, carry out	implement, effectuate
happen	eventuate, transpire
inform	apprise
make	render
send	transmit
think	deem
think, see, regard	envisage

(e) Use Concrete Rather Than Abstract Words

Concrete words such as "split decision" are easier to understand than abstractions such as "judicial dichotomy." Legal writers are likely to use abstract, overblown language in part because many of the cases that law students read during their first year reflect an older, overstuffed style that is all too easy to imitate. Legal writers must resist the old style.

Some common abstractions are simple words that can often be eliminated without loss of meaning, for example, "type," "kind," "manner," "state," "area," "matter," "factor," "system," and "nature."

1. The *central thrust* of plaintiff's legal *position* is dependent on *matters* having to do with three decisions of the United States Supreme Court.

Revised: Plaintiff's argument for summary judgment depends on three United States Supreme Court decisions.

2. The court may not abandon the traditional termination-at-will *manner* of analysis in order to apply a reasonableness *factor* in the *area* of non-employment contracts.

Revised: The court may not abandon the traditional termination-at-will analysis for non-employment contracts in order to apply the reasonableness analysis.

3. The above *arguments are likely to encounter two problems due to* the particular *kind of facts* in this case. (Abstract subject-verb-object: arguments encounter problems.)

Revised: Our client's delay and abusive manner weaken the good faith argument in this case. ("Delay and abusive manner" make specific what "kind of facts" are referred to.)

[*106*]

(f) Use Words That Are Consistent in Tone

All words have connotation (overtones of meaning) as well as denotation (explicit meaning). Since connotation contributes to tone, the word choices in a particular piece of legal writing should have compatible connotations. Many briefs contain glaring inconsistencies in tone, as in the following excerpt from a fact statement:

> A third-party park-sitter, unbeknownst to Plaintiff, contacted said Plaintiff's head with a wine bottle. Plaintiff now has two metal plates and twelve screws holding things together.

(g) Avoid Equivocations

Lawyers and law students often hesitate to make direct or dogmatic statements. To protect themselves or to reflect uncertainty, they use either equivocal or qualifying words that undermine their meaning. Typical words and phrases used in this way are: "it seems to indicate," "if practicable," "it would seem," "it may well be," and "it might be said that." If you are uncertain, state the reasons for your uncertainty.

(h) Use Unqualified Nouns, Adjectives, and Verbs

Many writers add modifiers to intensify or buttress poorly chosen nouns, adjectives, and verbs. The right word ordinarily needs no bolstering.

When the following modifiers are removed, emphasis falls naturally where it should: on the noun, adjective, or verb.

absolutely	nearly
actually	obviously
basically	particular
certain, certainly	plainly
clearly	practically
completely	pretty much
deepest	quite
extremely	really
frankly	so (as in "so great")
generally	sort of
given	surely
greatly	truly
in effect	various
kind of	very
more or less	virtually

1. The surface of the material *basically* was *very* rough and extremely discolored.

Revised: The surface of the material was coarse and blotched.

2. The tide was *obviously* faster than the owner's engineers had calculated, making the owner *clearly* liable for its *completely* inadequate construction plan.

Revised: The tide was faster than the owner's engineers had calculated, making the owner liable for inadequacy of its construction plan.

Words that convey absolute qualities must remain unqualified if they are to retain their meaning, for example, "perfect," "dead," "absolute," "equal," "essential," "matchless," "mortal," "universal," "supreme," and "unique."

(i) Use Few Literary Devices

A plain style is usually the best style. If you do wish to use figurative language, do so where it will not interfere with communication of substance. When you edit or revise, consider the sensory dimension of words. Omit rhyme ("however clever"), cacophony ("egalitarian documentation"), conspicuous alliteration ("fallibility of four factfinders"), and unintentional puns ("a case without appeal").

Clichés come readily to mind during writing. Thus a standard part of your revision should be to remove them or to renovate them. For example, you might play on the common cliché "adding insult to injury" by writing "adding insult to perjury," but remove such clichés as "height of absurdity," "day of reckoning," and "cold light of reason."

(j) Avoid Jargon From Other Fields

Words go in and out of fashion. Vague psychoanalytic terms, such as "interaction" and "supportive," were frequently used for a time before they gave way to computer jargon, such as "interface" and "input." Avoid word fads altogether. Words in fashion are quickly degraded;

their specific meaning disappears, leaving only a vague general meaning.

§ 5.3 A FEW BRIEF WORDS: REDUNDANCY IN LEGAL WRITING

As most lawyers know, redundant wording has a long and respectable past. Our Anglo-Saxon ancestors gave us word pairings, such as "safe and sound." After the Norman Invasion, French synonyms were added to the Middle English word pairs. Thus many legal terms have come to us in triplicate, for example, "give (Old English), devise (Old French) and bequeath (Old English)." Some word pairings are still commonly used, such as "acknowledge and confess," "act and deed," "deem and consider," "fit and proper,", "goods and chattels," "keep and maintain," "pardon and forgive," "shun and avoid," "aid and abet," "cease and desist," "fraud and deceit," and "null and void." Before automatically adopting an archaic word pairing, consider whether both words are needed.

Unnecessary word pairing continues to be a habit in modern English. If you think about each word you use, you will avoid redundancies such as the following.

basic fundamentals	telling revelation
basic starting point	terrible tragedy
false misrepresentation	true facts
final result	unexpected surprise

if and when	unless and until
sufficient enough	save and except

A more pervasive form of redundancy is the throw-away phrase, such as:

a certain amount of	as a matter of fact
due to the fact that	all intents and purposes
in case of	the nature of the case is
in regard to	the necessity of
the fact of the matter is	with reference to

Watch for these phrases when you edit, and gradually train yourself to omit them during initial drafting.

Many other unnecessary words litter professional prose, and many writing texts offer lists of those words. As an editing technique, ask the question, "Do I need this word?" for each word in your next few writing projects, and you will begin instinctively to pare away such unnecessary words and phrases as these:

Wordy	*Revised*
am hopeful that	hope
at that point in time	then
by means, reason, or virtue of	by
despite the fact that	although, even though
give recognition to	recognize
have knowledge of	know
in accordance with	by, under

in order to	to
in relation to	about
in the majority of instances	usually
is applicable to	applies to
is dependent on	depends on
make application to	apply to
make provision for	provide for
provides with an example of	exemplifies
until such time as	until

While redundancy wastes a reader's time, repetition of key words saves a reader's time. From sentence to sentence, key nouns and verbs should be repeated. The line between helpful repetition and redundancy is thin, but with experience the legal writer will develop a sense for where that line is.

§ 5.4   GLOSSARY OF WORDS COMMONLY MISUSED IN LEGAL WRITING

Every legal writer should regularly consult a standard usage text. This glossary is not intended as a substitute. Rather, it is intended as a law-oriented supplement to standard references such as those cited in the Selected References at the end of this *Nutshell*.

above, as in *above* theory. Usage experts acknowledge this use of *above* with a noun to be permissible but prefer reversed order (theory *above*) by analogy to other indicators of place (*e.g., below*). Use of *above* with a verb is more precise (*e.g., above*-mentioned theory, theory summarized *above*) because what has been done *above* is identified. All of these usages are to be preferred to *aforesaid* in legal prose.

abstruse, obtuse. *Abstruse* is an adjective meaning "hard to understand." *Obtuse* is an adjective meaning "dull, insensitive in perception or imagination, slow to understand." A lawyer's reasoning may be *abstruse* because the lawyer is *obtuse*.

accuse, accused, as in *The plaintiffs were accused of failing to maintain the premises in a safe condition.*

1. The preposition *of* is correct.

2. Use of *accuse* in relation to a civil fault is incorrect. In non-legal usage *accuse* means "to charge with a fault or an offense." In legal usage it has been limited to charging a crime.

adverse, averse. *Adverse* is an adjective meaning "against, opposed, harmful, or unfavorable," as in *adverse to the plaintiff's position*. *Averse* is an adjective meaning "unwilling, reluctant, or set against," with connotations of distaste or repugnance, as in *Law students are sometimes averse to rigorous writing exercises.*

affect, effect.

1. As nouns. *Effect* is probably the word you want to use. It means "result or accomplish-

[*113*]

ment." *Affect* (*af´fect*—accent on the first syllable) is a psychological term that you will probably never have occasion to use in legal prose. (It refers to the conscious subjective aspect of an emotion.)

2. As verbs. Confusion of the two words commonly occurs in their use as verbs. *Effect* means "to bring about, to accomplish." *Affect* (accent on the last syllable) means "to influence."

allege, allegation.

1. *Allege* is spelled without a "d" before the "g."

2. *Allege* means "to declare or assert without proof." Do not use it when you mean *contend* or *argue* in the sense of giving reasons for or against something.

alternate, alternative.

1. *Alternate* as an adjective means "by turns." The derived adverb has the same meaning, as in *Defendant's two lawyers sought to question witnesses alternately.*

Alternative as an adjective means "offering a choice between two or more possibilities." The derived abverb has the same meaning: *Appellant's counsel argued alternative theories—that there was no contract and that if there was, it was breached by the defendant,* or *She argued that there was no contract and, alternatively, that if there was a contract, it was breached by the defendant.*

2. *Alternative* as a noun also means "a choice between two or more incompatible possibilities," as in *There is no* [not *no other*] *alternative* or in *The only alternative is settlement or trial* (that is, the only choice is the choice between settlement or trial). The noun also has a secondary meaning, that is, one of the several incompatible possibilities to be chosen, as in these sentences: *The settlement alternative is unattractive* and *The only alternatives are settlement and trial.*

3. Do not use the adjective *alternative* as a synonym for *new, other,* or *revised.*

among, between. *Among* is precisely used to express a relation of more than two persons: *among the four parties. Between* ("by-twain") is precisely used to express a relation of two persons: *between the two parties.* Therefore, the common contractual language *among and between parties A, B, and C* is not a redundancy. It means: among A, B, and C; between A and B, B and C, and A and C. From its first use, however, *between* has extended to more than two things in some situations and is the only word for expressing the relation of a physical thing to many surrounding things, as in *the property between the three rivers.*

and/or. Avoid this confusing usage. *And/or* may be interpreted as (i) both *and* AND *or*; (ii) either *and* OR *or* but not both. In other expressions, the slash stands for the words "or" or "per." Therefore, *and/or* should carry the second meaning (ii). Because its usage is erratic, however, legal writers should state what is intended: *fined or imprisoned or both* rather than *fined and/or imprisoned*.

anticipate, expect. These words should not be used synonymously. Use *expect* to mean "to look for as likely to occur" or "to look for as necessary or proper," as in *We expect the judge to grant a continuance*. Use *anticipate* to mean "to forestall, to take steps beforehand, to use or enjoy in advance, to do something before someone else," as in *Opposing counsel anticipated our strategy and moved for a continuance*.

appeal. To *appeal* (verb) means "to seek review of a decision in a legal action as a matter of right." If review is not available as of right, but only within a court's discretion, then one *applies for a writ* (*e.g.*, of certiorari).

appellee, appellant. See **parties in litigation**.

argue, contend, maintain. Courts do not *contend, maintain* or *argue*. Counsel *contend* and *argue*. Courts *hold, decide, reason, state, suggest, imply, conclude*.

as. Do not use the conjunction *as* when you mean "since," "because," "when," or "while." Its broad and vague meanings can create confusion. For example, *As a potential work stoppage threatened to block the opening of school, the arbitrators revised the wording of the contract.* Does *as* mean "when," "because," or "while"?

as if, like. Do not use *like* in place of *as if*: *The judge proceeded as if* [not *like*] *counsel had raised no objection.*

as, like. *As*, as a conjunction, is used to introduce a clause (a verb must follow *as*): *Students must learn to think as lawyers do. Like*, as a preposition, is used for comparisons: *Students must learn to think like lawyers.*

as such, as in *The court limited the decision to subsequent cases; as such, the decision does not affect our case. Such* is here used as a pronoun. It should therefore have a referent. Its use seems most justified when a comparison is to be made, for example, *It was a prospective decision; as such it does not affect our case. As an indication of the court's attitude, however, it is significant.*

assume, assumption. *Assume* means "to accept as granted that something is true or accurate." Do not use the word or its derivatives

when you mean "conclude," that is, to accept
something on the basis of reasoning.

attorney, counsel, counselor, lawyer. The distinctions have been explained as follows: *Lawyer*
is a general term, designating one who practices
law. *Attorney* refers to one who has been desig-
nated to transact business for another (that is, a
lawyer who has a client). A *counsel* is one who
gives legal advice. *Counselor* means the same
thing as *counsel*; it is most commonly used in
court as a term of address. See also **counsel,
counselor**.

based on, as in *Based on this decision, our client may be held liable for a breach of contract.*
This use of *based on* is common but incorrect. In
the example, *based on* modifies *our client*, thus
suggesting that *our client was based on this decision.* To correct the example, substitute *given*
for *based on*. (Note also the use of *breach* as a
noun. Purists would object to the expression *for
breaching the contract*, although dictionaries
now bless the use of *breach* as a verb.)

basic, basically. *Basic* means "fundamental."
The derived adverb, *basically*, should not be used
as an introductory word without any clear meaning, as in these sentences: *Basically, I am reluctant to recommend that we go to trial*, and *Basically, the statute is not clearly drafted.*

basis, as in *on the basis of.* Single prepositions or other more precise phrases can often be
substituted for this jargon phrase, *e.g.*, substitute
under in *It is nowhere stated that entitlement
on the basis of section 416(h)(7)(A) must be full
entitlement.* Substitute *by* in *Our client will be
judged on the basis of the new standard.* Substitute *on* in *The case was presented to the court
on the basis of certified questions.*

between. See **among, between**.

blatant. *Blatant* means "noisy, clamorous, obtrusive." It is often used when *flagrant* is intended, as in this sentence: *This result is in blatant conflict with the purpose of the Act.* Even
the correct use of *flagrant*, meaning "gross,
openly evil," is usually overstatement or over-
argument in legal prose.

breach, as a verb. See **based on**.

by, as in *by January 15.* The phrase is ambiguous. Does it mean *before* January 15 or *on or
before* January 15? Say which you mean.

case.

1. *Case* signifies, among other things, a dispute regularly and properly before a court for
resolution. Do not personify *case*, as in *The Sutton case so held.* (Rather, write *In the Sutton
case, the court so held.*) Do not write *This case
presented itself to the court on certified ques-*

tions. (Rather, write *This case was presented to the court on certified questions.*)

2.　Do not use *where* with *case* when you mean *in which* or *wherein: The most significant case is United Labor, where the court so held.* Instead, use *in which the court so held.*

3.　Do not use *case* when you mean *court* or *opinion.* See **court** 4.

4.　*Case* may also refer to a dispute or other matter not yet before a court for resolution. Because the word can be used in the two different senses, it should be used with clear modifiers to avoid confusion. For example, if you use *this case* in a law office memorandum, it may not be clear whether you are referring to a decided *case* that you have just cited or to the client's *case* about which the memorandum is written. If you use *this case* in a brief, it might be taken as a reference to a decided *case* previously cited or to the *case* in which the argument is being presented. Here are some frequently used forms of reference that avoid such confusion. For decided cases: use an abbreviated part of the case title (for example, *Brinkly*) or use *that case* or *the cited case.* For your client's case: *the case before this court* or *our case. Case at hand* and *instant case* are also commonly used, but may seem pretentious.

5.　In a more general sense, *case* is used for a situation, a set of circumstances, an instance, an example, and other less clearly defined referents. It has been imbedded in trite phrases that have, at best, no meaning, or at worst, an ambiguous meaning, *e.g., in the case of, in any case.*　When tempted to use a phrase containing *case*, consider (a) whether the phrase is necessary, and (b) if it is, whether a more precise word can be substituted for *case.*

citation, cite.

1.　In legal writing, indications of authorities are called *citations*, not *references.*

2.　*Cite* is a verb.　It should not be used in place of *citation*, as in *The plaintiff's citations* [not *cites*] *are inaccurate.*

claim.　This word has a special meaning under federal civil procedure rule 8(a), relating to *claims for relief.*　More generally, it also means "to assert or demand a right or title to something."　Unfortunately, it is commonly used incorrectly for *allege, state, declare, argue, argument,* or *conclude.*　One student managed to squeeze most of these different meanings into one paragraph: *One claim [1] that could be made is that the Commission does not have the power to impose a sanction.　Plaintiff could also claim [2] that the action cannot lie since the complaint does not claim [3] any arrest or seizure of* *property and special injury, which the Washington court has held is necessary in any claim [4] for malicious prosecution.* Translations: [1]*argument,* [2]*argue,* [3]*allege* or *aver,* and [4]*claim*—correctly used in the special sense of civil procedure. Here is another misuse: *The court claimed that the minority position was erroneous. Claimed* should be *concluded* or some other verb. See **argue, contend, maintain.**

compare to, compare with. We *compare* one case *with* another (examine similarities and differences) but *compare* a cliché *to* a comfortable old shoe (liken one thing to another).

compose, comprise. *Compose* means "to make up" or "to constitute." *Comprise* means "to be composed of" or "to consist of." *The American Digest System comprises nine units and a current supplement* (or *is composed of*). *Nine units and a current supplement compose the American Digest System* (or *are comprised in*).

conclusions of law. See **find, finding.**

conform. A contract may *conform to* law or be *in conformity with* law. Goods may *conform to* description or be *in conformity with* description.

construction, interpretation. These words are commonly used interchangeably to refer to the process of determining the meaning of contracts and statutes. A useful distinction has been suggested, however, in 3 *Corbin on Contracts* 9 (1960): "[T]he word *interpretation* is commonly used with respect to language itself—to the symbols (the words and acts) of expression. . . . By 'interpretation of language' we determine what ideas that language induces in other persons. By 'construction of the contract' . . . we determine its legal operation—its effect upon the action of courts and administrative officials."

contain. Search for a more precise verb if you are tempted to say something like this: *The Rosenberg opinion contains several relevant factors that should be developed in our case.* (*identifies? suggests? summarizes* ?)

contend. See **argue, contend, maintain.**

continual, continuous. *Continual* means "frequently or closely repeated." *Continuous* means "without interruption."

contract. One is a party *to*, not *of*, a contract. But, does one *enter* or *enter into* a contract? The latter seems to be the correct usage (though the former occasionally appears in otherwise carefully written court opinions): one *enters* a transaction on the books but *enters into* an association.

counsel, counselor. Note the correct spelling for the words used to describe one who gives legal advice. Note also that *counsel* is the correct form for both singular and plural. See also **attorney, counsel, counselor, lawyer**.

court.

1. A court with more than one judge is an entity (*it*), not a collection of individuals (*they*). If the judges are not unanimous in deciding a case, then you may refer to *the majority of the court* and the *dissenting* (or *concurring*) *judges* or to *dissenters*. See **dissent**. You may also refer to the majority's decision as the decision of *the court* (or *the Court* if you are referring to the United States Supreme Court). If you are reporting a particular judge's view (for example, that of a concurring or dissenting judge), use *Judge* _____; for the United States Supreme Court and some state supreme courts, use *Justice* _____. (Note that *Mr. Justice* _____ is no longer used for United States Supreme Court justices. The "Mr." has been dropped in accordance with notice by Associate Justice Stevens to the clerk's office. *National Law Journal*, Dec. 1, 1980, at 55, col. 1, 2.)

2. Either *judge* or *court* may be used to refer to a court with a single judge, for example, for a trial court.

3. Do not substitute the name of a jurisdiction for *court*. For example, *California has held* is incorrect; it should be *the California court has held* if reference is to the highest court in the

state or *a California court has held* if the reference is to other than the highest court.

4.   Do not substitute *case* or *opinion* for *court* or *judge*. For example, *The Graham case so held* is incorrect; it should be *In the Graham case the California court so held*.

criteria. *Criteria* is a plural noun. The singular is *criterion*.

deals with, as in *The federal regulation specifically deals with "cooperation" in obtaining support.* This phrase is often a fuzzy substitute for a more descriptive verb. Here, for example, the writer may have meant that the regulation *defines "cooperation,"* or *specifies when "cooperation" may be required.* The more precise explanation should be provided.

decide, decision. See **hold, holding**.

deed, quitclaim deed, title.

1.   It is the *deed,* not the title that is *delivered and recorded.*

2.   *Quit*claim is correct, not *quick*claim. *Quitclaim* is not hyphenated.

defendant. See **parties in litigation**.

dicta, dictum.

1.   *Dicta* is plural; *a dictum* is singular.

2.   *Dicta* are statements in a court opinion that are not necessary to the court's resolution of the problem before it, or, stated in another way,

they are answers to questions not presented. Thus, the words *dicta* and *holdings* are mutually exclusive. Therefore, it is gross error to say that a court *held in dicta*; rather, a court *states in dicta*. If the correct characterization is in doubt, use an expression like *stated in what may be dicta* and explain the reason for doubt. *Binding dicta* is equally objectionable.

different.

1. Use *different from* rather than *different than* and you will usually be safe. Thus, a case may be *different from* a previously decided case.

2. Do not use "no" with *different from* as in this sentence: *The conclusion reached by the scholars is that the rule in defamation cases should be no different from the rule in other cases.* (Rather, *the rule in defamation cases should not be different from* or *should not differ from.*)

disinterested, uninterested. *Disinterested* means "free from bias and self-interest." *Uninterested* means "not interested or apathetic." The distinction must be observed in legal contexts. In an administrative proceeding, the hearing official must be *disinterested*; whether he or she is *uninterested* is usually not legally significant.

dissent. Do not use *dissent* as a substitute for *dissenters, dissenting judges,* or *dissenting* *opinion.* Examples: *The dissent based its conclusion on a fiction rather than on public policy.* (Rather, *The dissenters* [or *dissenting judges*] *based their conclusion on a fiction rather than on public policy.*) *The reasons for the differing views were detailed in the dissent.* (Rather, *The reasons for the differing views were detailed in the dissenting opinion.*) See also **court** 1.

doubtless, no doubt, undoubtedly. *Doubtless,* as an adverb, and *no doubt* have lost the literal sense of "without doubt." Now they merely suggest probability or concession, as in *The court doubtless considered the possibility* and *No doubt other opinions exist.* To express the absence of doubt, use *undoubtedly, without a doubt,* or *beyond a doubt.*

due to.

1. *Caused by, resulting from,* or *because of* will be more precise expressions than *due to* in such sentences as these: *The court allowed the tenant to recover for personal injuries due to the landlord's negligent maintenance.* (Rather, *for personal injuries resulting from the landlord's negligent maintenance.*) *This reasoning will become more appealing in light of the injustice suffered by litigants due to extensive court delays.* (Rather, *in light of injustice suf-*

fered by litigants because of extensive court delays.)

2. *Due to* is often superfluous in the statement of a reason, as in this sentence: *The reason for distinguishing the cases may be due to different characteristics of the two types of vehicles.* (Rather, *The reason for distinguishing the cases may be the different characteristics of the two types of vehicles.*)

easy, easily, readily. These are often whistling-in-the-dark words, as in *It is easy to argue that* or *It could readily be argued that.* Avoid such usages. State what you mean: That a point could be *persuasively* or *authoritatively* so argued? That opposing counsel may be expected to so argue? That a careless attorney might so argue?

effect. See **affect**.

establishment. This word is often either incorrectly used or used in an awkward way (even though used correctly to mean "an act of establishing" or "state of being established"). Examples: *The establishment of the disclosure violation may be difficult.* (Rather, *Establishing the disclosure violation may be difficult.*) *Plaintiff's claim for benefits was barred by Mary Lou's establishment of her claim as Joseph's legal widow.* (Rather, *The claim was barred by Mary Lou's having previously established her*

claim.) *The Secretary is charged with establishment of standards for state programs.*
(Rather, *The Secretary is charged with drafting*
or *adopting standards.*) *The survey revealed
that many deserting fathers could afford to
make child support payments but do not—either through lack of establishment or lack of
enforcement of obligations.* (Rather, *either because their duty is not established or is not en-
forced.*)

expect. See **anticipate, expect**.

explicit, implicit. Use these words in their literal, not their colloquial sense. *Implicit* means
"implied, understood though unexpressed." Do
not use it to mean "absolute, full, or complete,"
as in *implicit obedience*. The antithesis of *implicit* is *explicit*. Do not use it to mean "absolute, full or complete," as in *the one explicit payment* or in *that explicit group of people*. The
opposites, *implied* and *expressed*, have not acquired colloquial meanings and so may be the
wiser choices for the legal writer.

fact.

1. The line between *fact* and *rule* may be in-
distinct, but it should not be ignored, as in this
sentence: *This result is a reaction to the fact
that the parent-child relationship alone is not
sufficient to impute liability.* The writer was
clearly noting the effect of a *rule*, not a *fact*.

2. *The true facts are stated in the record.*
Strike *true*. *Facts* are true by definition. But a
statement of facts may be untrue or inaccurate.

3. See **find, finding**.

farther, further. Distinctions between these
two words seem to be disappearing. You will not
be faulted, however, if you confine your use of
farther to describe physical distance. Thus, *The
court reasoned further that . . .*

feel, as in *The court felt that the result was
justified* or in *I feel . . .*

1. A *court* does not *feel*, and we ordinarily
cannot know how the *judges feel* about a case.
Search for a more precise verb.

2. Search for a more precise word also if you
are tempted to say, "I feel . . ." Usually you
will realize that you *conclude, believe, assume,*
or *infer.* Use *feel* only if you are making an intuitive or emotional statement.

few, fewer, less.

1. *Fewer* means "a smaller number," as in
fewer people (not *less people*) and *fewer mis-
takes, fewer words.* *Less* as a comparative
means "a smaller amount of," as in *less pay.*

2. Use *comparatively few,* not *a comparative
few* or *the comparative few* (neither of which
makes sense).

find, finding. Courts may *find facts*. *Findings of fact* are a court's determinations of the facts. The *findings* may be included in a document stating those factual determinations and also stating legal conclusions. The title of the document is "Findings of Fact and Conclusions of Law." The document, signed by the judge, is commonly required in cases tried before a judge without a jury.

guilty, liable. *Guilty* carries stronger implications of blameworthiness than *liable*. It implies consciousness of crime or moral wrong. Hence, it is appropriate to say that a person is *guilty of a crime* but *liable for negligence* (or other civil fault).

heavily, as in *The court relied heavily on distinguishable precedents*. The word is trite and imprecise. Did the court rely *exclusively*? *primarily*? *in part*?

hold, holding, decide, decision.

1. *Holding* refers to the result reached by a court in resolving a case regularly and properly before it. That result may also be called a *decision* (though *decision* may also be used in a more general sense). A *holding* is unique because it can refer only to the result on the facts and for the parties in a particular case. Neither *holding* nor *decision* should be used to refer to a *rule*, which is a more general statement that explains

many cases. (But see **rule, ruling** 3.) Example:
*The court applied the rule that a violation of a
zoning ordinance is not an encumbrance that
renders title unmarketable. It then held that
the violation of the Seattle ordinance that re-
stricted use of the building on the defendant's
property did not render the defendant's title
unmarketable. Holding* may also refer to the
result in a case in a procedural sense, as in *The
court's holding that the complaint should be
dismissed was in error.* These observations apply also to the verbs *hold* and *decide.*

2. Courts *hold*. Rules do not. Therefore use
of *holds* in the following sentence is both wrong
and redundant: *Our client's position will be af-
fected by the rule that holds that evidence of remarriage must not be admitted.*

3. Since *hold* and *holding* have a technical
meaning, their use in general or non-technical
senses should be avoided, as in *This argument
does not hold* or in *The court holds [reasons]
that such information would mislead the jury.*

idea. This word is used to express vaguely a
number of "ideas" that should be more precisely
identified, as in these sentences: *In McDonald
the court directly addressed the assumption of
risk idea.* (Assumption of risk *defense*?) *The
Washington court deals unfavorably with the
idea concerning public policy.* (Public policy

argument?) *Analysis of the idea suggests that the Washington court would allow disclosure.* (Analysis of the *rationale*? the *criticism*?)

impact. As a noun *impact* means "the forceful striking of one thing against another, a collision." Do not use it figuratively to mean "effect or influence" as in this sentence: *The impact of the court's decision cannot be predicted at this time.*

implicit. See **explicit, implicit.**

imply, infer. *Imply* means "to suggest or to say indirectly." *Infer* means "to surmise or to draw a conclusion from something written or spoken by someone else." Thus, a court may *imply* a conclusion in its opinion, but a reader will *infer* the conclusion from the court's opinion.

in terms of. This phrase is commonly used as a substitute for a precise identification of relationship or as a substitute for such prepositions as *at, by, as,* or *for.* The phrase is correctly used when one thing is being expressed *in terms of* another thing, as when a rule is discussed *in terms of* its economic effect. The phrase is loosely or incorrectly used in the following sentences: *This policy argument is strong in terms of our client's case.* (Is a strong argument for our client? Or for the opposition?) *If the doctor's words are construed in terms of a guarantee, the result will be different.* (Construed *as* a guarantee?)

interpretation.   See **construction**.

issue.

1.   An *issue* is a question that can be answered in more than one way, a point of dispute or controversy.   *Issue* should not be used vaguely or unnecessarily.   For example, in *The issue of assignment is not disputed*, the word is used improperly.   What is not disputed?   The *existence* of an assignment?   The *validity* of an assignment?   In the following sentence, the introductory phrase is used unnecessarily: *The issue of whether the assignment was valid was decided without reference to the controlling precedent.* The sentence may be correctly written without *"The issue of"* or even more concisely thus, *The assignment issue was decided without reference to the controlling precedent*, if the *issue* has been previously stated.

2.   The following phrases should be distinguished: *In issue* refers to points that are in controversy or disputed, particularly those issues that are properly before a court.   *At issue* refers to issues that are ready for decision, ready to go to the trier of fact (judge or jury).

it is, there is.   Sentences beginning with these words can often be rewritten more concisely and more directly.   For example, *It is uncertain as to which procedure the agency must follow* can be more directly written as *Which procedure the* *agency must follow is uncertain.* The sentence *There is no provision in the statute for rescission if the notice is given* can be more concisely written as *The statute does not provide for rescission if the notice is given.*

judge, justice. See **court** 1.

judgment. When used to mean the terminal decision or document in litigation, *judgment* is spelled without the middle "e" in American legal materials, although use of that "e" ("judgement") is an accepted variant spelling in English legal materials and in other settings.

jurisdiction. This word is commonly used in two senses: to refer to a court system (for example, the federal *jurisdiction*) and to refer to the power of a court or a court system to hear and decide particular disputes. Do not use *jurisdiction* in the former sense when you are actually referring to a particular court. See **court** 3.

lawyer. See **attorney, counsel, counselor, lawyer**.

less. See **few, fewer, less**.

liable, liability.

1. See **guilty**.

2. *Liability* is *imposed on* a party to litigation, not *fastened on, placed on,* or *procured.*

like. See **as, like** and **as if, like.**

likely.

1.   When *likely* is used as an adverb, it ought to be modified by a qualifying word like *quite, very*, or *most* as in *A decision will most likely be given within ten days.*

2.   The colloquial misuse of *likely* instead of *probably* in the following examples is becoming too common: *There will likely be a change* and *Its validity as a contract will likely be challenged.*

ludicrous, as in *It is ludicrous to say that Congress intended this result in such a small class of cases.*   This word means "inept, foolish, or exaggerated to the point of absurdity."   To so characterize an opposing counsel's argument or a court's rationale is to overargue or overstate.

maintain.   See **argue**.

memoranda, memorandum.   The singular form is *memorandum.*

no doubt.   See **doubtless, no doubt, undoubtedly**.

obtuse.   See **abstruse, obtuse**.

opinion.   A court *opinion* is the official written statement of a court's decision in a case and its reasons for reaching the decision.   For appropriate usage, see **court** 4.

oral, verbal.   *Oral* means "spoken or uttered." *Verbal* means "with words or consisting of words, either written or spoken."   Thus, *whether* *in writing or verbal* makes no sense; it should be *whether written or oral.*

overrule, reverse.

1. A court *overrules* its prior decisions and the decisions of lower courts within its jurisdiction. A court *reverses* a lower court judgment in the specific case before it, for example, *After holding that the precedent on which the lower court relied should be overruled, the supreme court held that the judgment for plaintiff should be reversed.* See also **rule, ruling** 3.

2. A decision is *overruled* only when the subsequent decision is directly contrary to the earlier decision. If the later decision is not directly contrary, then the earlier decision may be *limited* or *modified.*

3. Dicta are *disapproved,* not *overruled.*

4. Courts also *overrule* objections.

5. *Overrule* is sometimes used with respect to motions (applications to courts for orders), but *deny* seems to be the correct verb.

parol, parole. *Parol* is a noun or adjective meaning *oral,* as in *parol evidence* or *parol lease* or *proof by parol.* *Parole* is a noun or a verb meaning *conditional release of a prisoner.*

parties in litigation.

1. A suit may be commenced by a *plaintiff* or by a *petitioner,* the latter term being used in

some equity proceedings and in applications for extraordinary writs, such as mandamus or quo warranto. The party sued is a *defendant* (spelled with an "*a*nt," not an "*e*nt").

2. One who appeals as a matter of right will usually be called the *appellant.* The other party may be a *respondent* (spelled with an "*e*nt," not an "*a*nt") or an *appellee* ; the choice apparently depends on which term happens to be used in the controlling rules or statutes. One who seeks review that is discretionary with a court (see **appeal**) is a *petitioner.*

3. In text, capitalize the title of a party (*e. g.,* plaintiff, appellant) only if you are using it as a formal title or as a substitute for a proper name, omitting "the," for example: *Plaintiff telephoned Defendant [or Defendant Jones] several times but failed to reach her.* But: *The plaintiff telephoned the defendant several times.*

petitioner, plaintiff. See **parties in litigation.**

precedence, precedents. *Precedents* are court decisions that may be followed by courts in subsequent cases presenting the same legal problem. *Precedence* means "priority, the fact of preceding in time."

principal, principle. Remember the different spellings for three different meanings: *The prin-*

cipal [primary] *objection to the liability princi-ple* [general and fundamental rule] *is that the agent's principal* [one who employs another to act] *escapes all liability.*

question of. This phrase is often used to introduce something that is not a question or that should be stated as a "whether" clause. For example, *The question of protective payments depends on two determinations.* Either a more precise word should be selected (*the propriety of protective payments* or *the need for protective payments*) or the question should be stated, for example: *Whether protective payments should be made depends on two determinations.* Or, if the question has been previously stated, then, *The answer to the protective payment question depends on two determinations.*

quitclaim deed. See **deed**.

quote. Do not use this verb for the noun *quotation*. For example, *Both attorneys and law students tend to use too many quotes* [should be *quotations*] *in their briefs.*

re. *Re* means *in the matter of.* It is correctly used in the case title for certain kinds of legal proceedings (*In re* Jones) or in a non-textual introductory statement for a letter to identify the subject matter (preceding the text of the letter, thus: *Re: Jones v. Allen*). In text, use *regarding, about,* or *concerning,* for example, *I am* *writing to you about the appeal in the Jones case.*

respective, respectively. Do not use these words unnecessarily, as in *The lawyers presented their respective theories in extended oral arguments.* Rather, use them when necessary to clarify the relationships between sets of things and sets of their modifiers: *Under the will, John, Ann, and Gertrude respectively are to receive the antique shop, the farm, and the residue.* (This sentence is simpler than the alternative: Under the will, John is to receive the antique shop, Ann is to receive the farm, and Gertrude is to receive the residue.)

response, as in **in response to.** This phrase is often used incorrectly without a verb, as in the following sentences: *The regulations were [adopted] in response to the problem created by lack of definitions. Board Letter No. 829 was [written] in response to an inquiry about disclosure of a security interest in all after-acquired property.*

rule, ruling.

1. See **hold, holding.**

2. Give thought to selection of a precise verb in describing what a court does with reference to a rule. For example, rules may be *reaffirmed* (if previously applied by the same court), *adopted, accepted,* or *stated.* Use of *laid down, set down,*

or *set forth* normally reflects inexperience in legal writing.

3. **The court reversed the rule** is incorrect. *Judgments,* not *rules,* get reversed. (*Rules* are *no longer followed.*) A court's *ruling,* on the other hand, may be *reversed.* A *ruling* is a court's determination or order made during litigation, as in deciding pre-trial motions or points during trial. For example, a court may apply the hearsay *rule* in *ruling* that the evidence would not be admitted.

tenant, tenet. Do not confuse the spellings. A *tenant* occupies rented premises. A *tenet* is a doctrine regarded as true, particularly by a group.

there is. See **it is.**

this. This word accounts for much fuzzy legal writing. It is used to refer indefinitely to entire paragraphs of a preceding discussion. It is used to refer to ideas, arguments, reasoning, or things not previously mentioned. Avoid such indefinite references by following the simple rule never to use "this" without adding a word that identifies what "this" refers to. For example, *This [rule] opens the way for indiscriminate seizure. This [conclusion] is further substantiated in a case decided last year. This [lack of distinction] is what leads me to conclude that the Harold decision will be controlling. In 1960 the statute* *was amended; this [amendment] was intended to broaden the statute to cover new types of contracts.* (Better: *In 1960 the statute was amended to extend its coverage to new types of contracts.*)

title. See **deed**.

undoubtedly. See **doubtless, no doubt, undoubtedly**.

unique. *Unique* is an adjective meaning one of a kind. Do not use it to mean *unusual* or *remarkable*. A case is either *unique* or it is *not unique* : it cannot be *somewhat unique* or *most unique*.

verbal. See **oral, verbal**.

CHAPTER 6

THE TOTAL PRODUCT: ADVISORY LETTERS TO LAY PERSONS; OFFICE RESEARCH MEMORANDA

§ 6.1   INTRODUCTION

This chapter discusses two basic forms of advisory writing, that is, letters to clients and office research memoranda.   It introduces the problems of communicating with lay persons and suggests techniques for solving those problems.   It explains special features of office memoranda (described generally in Chapter 1) and suggests techniques for writing parts of an office memorandum.   Finally, this chapter suggests ways of combining these techniques with effective practices described in preceding chapters.

§ 6.2   WRITING FOR A LAY AUDIENCE

Lawyers write to clients to give answers to legal questions and to describe possible courses of action and attendant risks.   Most clients are lay persons, that is, they do not have special knowledge of the law, its concepts, and its terminology.   Because the lawyer should write for the client's benefit and understanding, writing an advisory letter to a client can be a difficult writing task. The first step is to recognize the problem.

Before beginning to write a letter to a client, ask these questions: What can I assume this client knows? Can I assume some or no acquaintance with the law? How can I accommodate my language and writing style to this reader without sounding condescending? Then write with the answers to those questions constantly in mind. Follow these additional guidelines:

Be direct. Answer the client's questions directly, and give advice or recommendations within the first few sentences. If direct answers and advice cannot be given, say so, and explain why. If you cannot provide an answer, admit it; do not try to bluff.

Be complete. State completely any advice or recommendations for action. State the facts upon which you base your answers and advice. This will allow your client to judge whether you are acting on complete and accurate information.

If the purpose of the letter is to weigh risks or courses of action, as in litigation, then consider theories of liability, possible damages, and probability of winning. Both the client's case and the opposing case should be outlined and fairly weighed. Give reasons in language the client can understand.

Be clear. Use plain language instead of technical terms. That is more difficult than may at first appear. In 1977 the New York legislature adopted a "plain language" law requiring clarity in form contracts used in consumer transactions. Six other state legislatures have now adopted similar laws requiring that such contracts be clearly written with commonly used words and appropriate sections and headings. The plain language crusade has met with resistance among lawyers and for good reasons. Lawyers cannot be expected to write all legal documents plainly enough for all persons to understand. The significant message from the plain language movement, however, is that documents such as mortgage and insurance forms should be understandable to the lay reader.

The message in this section is that lawyers' letters should be understandable, too. The following principles, developed as a part of the plain language movement, may aid in reaching that end:

(i) Words and phrases with which a lay reader is probably unfamiliar should be replaced with familiar words whenever this may be done without loss of meaning. For example, instead of "voir dire," write "questioning of prospective jurors"; instead of "statute of frauds," write "a statute that requires some contracts to be written."

(ii) Technical terms and terms of art should be defined or illustrated or both. If a definition would be too complex and difficult for a lay reader, an example should be used instead.

(iii) Terms with both legal and common meanings (for example "privilege") should be avoided or the differing meanings should be clearly identified.

(iv) To write plainly about the law, legal writers may sometimes have to sacrifice brevity, as in the examples given above for the first guideline.

Be specific.   Give exact times, costs, and other important information whenever possible. If exact information cannot be provided, explain why, and state when it will or may be available.

Be brief when the subject matter permits. Short letters need no apology. Do not pad a short letter. Omit legal analysis that does not directly explain your answer. Omit unnecessary expressions, such as "I would like to inquire about" (just inquire) and "we regret to inform you that" (just inform).

Be realistic.   Unless you are writing a formal opinion letter, leave out case analysis, obscure statutory language, and citations of authority. Of course, some clients may want this information as the basis for evaluation of the lawyer's answer or for assurance of lawyer-like consideration of the problem. For most clients, however, citations will be indecipherable. Before including case analysis or citations of authority, ask yourself whether your client will want to have and will understand this information.

Be objective. Lawyers sometimes argue their cases in letters to clients as an unconscious "warm-up" exercise before addressing the court. Such argument may have the unhappy effect of leading a client to expect more than the lawyer can deliver. Advisory writing may be argumentative at times, but the argument should have a specific, defensible purpose (*i.e.*, to persuade a client to give up a law suit or to change settlement terms).

Be considerate. Your client is someone with a problem. Try to solve that problem in a sincere and humane way. This requires careful control of tone. Do not joke about the severity or the insignificance of the client's problems. Keep the same level of formality throughout the letter. Do not begin with "Dear Charlie" and close with "Very truly yours, Bickerstaff, Edgewater, and Ransom." Do not try to impress your clients by using a formal or pompous tone, obscure reasoning, difficult legal terms, or pompous phrases, such as "preposterous on its face," "with matters in this recumbent posture," "a date certain," and "purports to know." Your letterhead and bill will impress them enough.

EXAMPLES:

1. *Mixed tone* (formal and colloquial): While no advantage to deletion of the provision is apparent, its deletion would not be the end of the world. I shall by separate cover provide for your perusal other illustrative provisions.

Revised: To omit the provision will do no harm that I can see. I will send other similar provisions to you in a separate letter. (Or: Next week I will send other similar provisions to you.)

2. *Wordy and indirect*: This will reply to your written inquiry of August 10, 1980, concerning certain aspects of your purchase. My delay in responding is due to overwhelming work for other clients. After extensive research, I am now able to consider the issues that you raise in the order that they occur in the letter.

Revised: In response to your August 10 inquiry, I have researched your problem and will answer your questions in the order you ask them.

3. *Indirect*: The following discussion addresses a concern raised by Ms. McGuire during your recent claims review. It was suggested that some discrepancy might possibly exist.

Revised: During your recent claims review, Ms. McGuire suggested that a discrepancy exists.

4. *Stilted wording*: The following basic principles must be considered so that the rationale for careful utilization of medical records can be appreciated.

Note: Will the client want to "appreciate the rationale?"

Revised : Medical records must be used carefully for the following reasons.

5. *Mixed metaphors* : Give me a call when you have digested this letter, and we can move ahead with the next step.

Revised : Please call when you are ready to proceed.

§ 6.3 OFFICE RESEARCH MEMORANDA

(a) Purposes

The office research memorandum is the basic document used in law offices. Its general purpose is to provide an analysis of a problem as the basis for giving advice or making decisions about the problem.

A memorandum should be written to serve the specific purpose for which it is requested. For example, an attorney may request a memorandum as the basis for:

(i) Considering whether to accept a case;

(ii) Preparing to meet with the client to obtain additional facts about the client's problem;

(iii) Preparing to advise a client on which of several courses of action to take;

(iv) Preparing for negotiations with the client's adversary;

(v) Preparing to draft a settlement agreement or other contract;

(vi) Preparing to draft a pleading or a discovery document;

(vii) Preparing for trial; or

(viii) Preparing for an appeal or other review of a court decision.

Even though preparation for settlement, trial, or appeal may not be the immediate purpose for a memorandum request, the memorandum discussion may have to be written with these future possibilities in mind.

Usually a memorandum will be written for another lawyer, such as a senior partner or associate. Sometimes, however, memoranda will be written for or shared with other professionals, such as accountants or trust officers. The prospective readers and the specific purposes of a memorandum should be identified as early in the research and writing process as possible to permit development of a solution responsive to the audience and purposes.

(b) Writing the Questions Presented

(1) Introduction

Identification of questions presented by a legal problem is the key to effective analysis. Sometimes questions will be clearly and precisely identified by the person who requests a research memorandum. More often, precise identification

[*150*]

comes slowly as a product of research, analysis of authorities, and reflective thinking.

Once questions are mentally identified, effective phrasing of them presents another challenge: how best to communicate the writer's understanding of the questions precisely and concisely to the reader. That is the subject of this subsection.

(2) Draft the Ultimate Question

To return to the beginning, think first about what we will call the "ultimate question"—the general question that prompts the request for a memorandum. The ultimate question may be as general as this: Can our client be liable under any theory for failure to arrange for transfer of his fire insurance for the benefit of the buyer of the client's warehouse that was later destroyed by fire? Or, it may be as specific as this: Whether evidence of plaintiff's remarriage is admissible in an action for wrongful death of a spouse. If the ultimate question is not clearly stated for you, try to draft a statement as soon as you begin work on a problem.

(3) Incorporate Key Facts

Questions should be meaningful standing alone. The readers should not have to read the full statement of facts in order to understand the

questions. Questions will be meaningful in that
sense if they are stated in terms of the facts of
the problem, not phrased in the abstract. Compare the following abstract question with the
questions stated in the preceding paragraph:

> Whether a promise to arrange for transfer of a
> fire insurance policy is enforceable.

If you use subquestions, each subquestion may
incorporate the facts peculiarly significant to that
subquestion. This practice will reduce the number of facts to be incorporated in the primary
question. The questions should state facts and
not legal conclusions.

Generally, when several facts are included in a
single issue sentence, the law is stated before the
facts. If the subject matter permits, the facts
should be arranged from the most general to the
most particular. The question itself should thus
move from the general area of law, at the beginning, to the most particular fact, at the end.

The question should include only the key facts.
Dates, amounts, locations, and other details
would ordinarily not be necessary, since they will
be supplied in a following Statement of Facts. If
the key facts are numerous, a preliminary factual
summary may be necessary to avoid an overlong
question statement. For example:

> Our client sold a warehouse that was later de-
> stroyed by fire. The buyer alleges that at the time
> the sale was closed, our client promised to arrange

for transfer of his fire insurance policy for the benefit of the buyer.

Question: May the client be liable to the buyer
for the full loss for failing to perform the alleged
promise?

(4) Use Subquestions Effectively

Formulation of more specific subquestions will
often be necessary as research and analysis progress. Writing and rewriting these questions
will often advance understanding of the problem
and promote reasoning to reliable conclusions.

Ordinarily, the more specifically the questions
can be stated, the more clearly and precisely they
can be discussed. A problem can be subdivided
into so many specific questions, however, that
both the reader and the writer become confused.
Guard against possible confusion by asking
whether your questions are related and whether
the relationships are apparent. Guard against
your reader's possible confusion by asking whether numerous subquestions will prevent a unified
view of the problem.

The form and style of questions will vary with
the subject matter, as illustrated by the examples
in the preceding paragraphs of this section and in
Chapters 2 and 7. Note, however, that a single
subquestion is never used. If there is a subquestion *a*, then there is a subquestion *b*. The existence of at least two subquestions follows from

the logic of division: If something is divided into parts, there must be at least two parts. When a primary question is stated with a single "sub-question," either the subquestion is a more specific restatement of the primary question or it is one of two or more subquestions. If you are tempted to state a single subquestion, decide which you must do: substitute the more specific formulation for the primary question or identify and state the other parts of the whole.

(5) Revise

Expect to revise your issue statements several times, including a final revision when you have finished writing the entire memorandum. Many of the suggestions for revision of sentences appearing in Chapter 4 will be useful in revising question statements.

(c) Writing the Brief Answer

This answer must be short. Answer each question in one sentence if possible. Cite precedents only if they are the crux of the problem. Although the Brief Answer appears before the Discussion section, it is often written after the Discussion section is in final or nearly final form. The clear understanding required for a succinct answer may come only with the discipline of writing a detailed Discussion.

(d) Writing the Statement of Facts

The Statement of Facts sets forth the basis of the legal problem. It tells the reader what happened, when, how, and to whom. No conclusions are reached. Editorial comments or evaluations of events are reserved for the Discussion section.

Facts should be presented so that the reader will understand on first reading and remember the key facts while reading the Discussion section. The facts should be stated in simple language without distortion or bias. The distinction between alleged facts and established facts should be observed through use of appropriate verbs, such as "alleged," "testified," "found by the court." Significant questions of fact should be signalled by mention of inconsistent information.

The two most common orders for fact statements are chronological and topical. Chronological order is most frequently used. The key facts are stated in the first sentence or two to orient the reader (that is, what happened, when, where, to whom). Then the events are narrated. Paragraphs in a chronological fact statement may be opened with relevant dates to make the chronology clear.

Topical order may be needed to organize a complex set of facts. Topic headings may then be used to identify shifts in topic. Be careful to in-

troduce and conclude this type of fact summary
and to provide explicit transitions and headings.
Topical order is common for multi-party problems
(for example, litigation involving several cross-
claims or numerous defendants) requiring that relationships among the parties be discussed sepa-
rately.

Many of the suggestions for revision of
sentences that appear in Chapter 4 are useful in
revising fact statements, as illustrated in the following example.

Unclear Statement of Facts:

The plaintiffs were general partners of a broker-
age firm that was liquidated and its assets transferred to defendant Cheerios, a partnership, and as
part of the transaction, Cheerios sold to plaintiffs
general and limited partnership units of Cheerios.
The plaintiffs alleged a violation by Cheerios of the
antifraud provisions of the federal securities statutes, which violation resulted in plaintiffs having
purchased their partnership interests for more than
they were allegedly worth.

Revised and Clarified:

The plaintiffs were general partners of a broker-
age firm that was liquidated.[1] The firm's assets
were transferred to defendant Cheerios, *also*[2] a
partnership. As *part of the transaction*,[2] *Cheerios
sold general and limited partnership units*[3] of
Cheerios to the plaintiffs. The plaintiffs *alleged
that Cheerios violated*[4] the antifraud provision of
the federal securities statutes. They *further alleged*[5] *that* this *violation* resulted in their purchase

[*156*]

of partnership interests for more than they were allegedly worth.

[1] One idea per sentence.

[2] Transitional words.

[3] Normal word order restored.

[4] Active, not passive, voice.

[5] Parallelism (fourth and fifth sentences).

(e) Writing the Discussion

(1) Write About the Particular Problem

A memorandum will usually be the basis for an attempt to resolve a particular dispute. Therefore, the law discussed should be clearly related to the particular facts of the dispute.

(2) Express Your Analysis and Conclusions Objectively

The purpose of an office memorandum is to explore the possible solutions to a legal problem. Exploration requires objectivity. The objective writer must explain the arguments that could be made for each side of the dispute and then assess their relative strengths.

The law student or beginning lawyer may have trouble writing objectively because the objective style is unfamiliar at first. All writers want to express feelings and opinions, especially if they have strongly held views. The process of researching and analyzing a problem often leads the researcher to strongly held opinions. One reason for this is that a legal problem usually requires inductive reasoning: the researcher gathers particulars in order to arrive at a generalization. Legal writing, however, generally requires a deductive format: the conclusion (generalization) is presented first, followed by statement of the analysis (contributing particulars). The use of deductive structure may cause the writer to try to prove favored generalizations and thus become argumentative. Memorandum writers must correct these argumentative tendencies if they are to lead the reader to an objective understanding of the problem.

(3) Write With Your Reader in Mind

For most office memoranda, the audience will be a lawyer. In this most common situation, you are speaking as a specialist to a specialist. Keep in mind, however, that you probably know more about the subject you have just researched than does the reader for whom you write. Provide the necessary background for understanding by explaining basic propositions and technical terms with which the reader may not be familiar or which the reader may not immediately recall.

In writing for a lawyer, a legal writer can take advantage of many shortcuts in communication. Legal terms of art and legal analysis will be readily understood, freeing the writer from detailed explanation. This license should not be abused, however, by using esoteric diction or jargon, by failing to provide logical connections between ideas because they seem "obvious," or by displaying high-sounding legal notions that are irrelevant to the subject.

If prospective readers are non-lawyers, then keep in mind the level of legal knowledge of the reader. Consider the suggestions about writing for lay persons that appear in the first section of this chapter.

(4) Be Conservative in Style and Tone

Express personal style primarily by sentence structures, not by idiosyncratic diction or by colloquialism. Colloquialism is easy to misinterpret and difficult to control in terms of tone and effect. A colloquial tone distracts from the information being conveyed. Avoid idiosyncratic expressions, such as *"early on* in the deposition," "an *outrageous* position," and *"on the order of* $110,000 in bonds."

The memorandum writer's tone should be unobtrusive so that the information is highlighted. A matter-of-fact tone is achieved by a straightforward, unequivocal declaration of findings and conclusions, without apologies or unnecessary qualifications.

(5) Be Selective in Using Quotations

Paraphrase judicial language rather than quoting at length. Isolate the relevant judicial language, quote it directly with necessary context, and paraphrase the rest. The reader should not have to decide what part of a long quotation is important.

(6) Use Headings and a Practical Format

The whole writing should be easy to use for quick reference. Divisions should be clearly marked; sections should be easy to locate.

Topic headings should be used for major divisions of any legal document of more than two or three pages. Subheadings may also be used to identify the topic of a paragraph or block of paragraphs, thereby reinforcing the traditional topic sentence.

In writing headings, remember the purposes to be served. Proper use of headings (i) assists the writer in organizing the document, (ii) assists the reader in understanding the writer's organization, (iii) assists the reader in referring back to matters covered in the document, (iv) assists the writer in making transitions between topics, and (v) informs the reader of a topic change.

Following are suggestions for form:

(i) Topic headings should be short to help the reader locate information quickly.

(ii) Form should be consistent: Use either complete sentences or topic summaries, but do not switch back and forth. The questions presented may be effective headings.

(iii) All words in fragmentary topic headings should begin with capital letters except prepositions (such as "of," "in"), articles (such as "a," "the"), and conjunctions of four letters or fewer (such as "and," "but").

(iv) Fragmentary topic headings are not punctuated.

(v) A colon is used for compound topic headings, for example: *The Basics: When Partition is Available.*

(vi) Headings are customarily underlined.

(f) Writing the Conclusion

The Conclusion may be used to tie together the answers already expressed for several questions presented. It may be used to state recommendations for handling a matter. It should not be a repetition of the Brief Answer, but it may parallel the Brief Answer. For example, the conclusion may provide more detailed explanations of reasoning summarily stated in the Brief Answer. Whatever its content, it should summarize. It should not introduce new authorities or new information about authorities covered in the Discussion.

§ 6.4 THE FINAL TOUCH

As every experienced writer knows, the first draft is never good enough. Revision is essential. Even a short letter should be reviewed for clarity, for ease of reading, for conciseness, and for errors. Extensive memoranda or briefs should be revised or rewritten several times. If the client can afford only one draft, then the lawyer must draft with extra care and review that draft conscientiously before final typing. If the pressure of time prevents the original writer from revising, someone else should review the work.

If the original drafter is able to revise, then the work should be put away for at least one day before revision. The lapse of time will allow the writer to return to the draft with greater detachment and a fresher eye.

During revision, the writer should review paragraphs and paragraph blocks to make sure that the topics are clearly indicated and well supported in the body of the paragraphs. The logical sequence of topics should be checked. The writer should review for adequate, informative transitions between paragraphs and sections. Sentences should be reviewed for readability and precision. For troublesome sentences, use the simple method for revision described in Chapter 4. After paragraphs and sentences have been re-examined, check for concise, parallel headings and subheadings. With dictated writing, it is especially important for the writer to see how paragraphs and sections look when typed.

As part of the revision, the writer should read the whole for uniform style and for consistency in wording and tone. Every citation and quotation should be checked against the original. Whenever possible, the writer should have someone else read for comprehensibility of sentences, usage, punctuation, and spelling. Although misspellings and typographical errors may provide comic relief to your reader, they do so at your expense. One lawyer learned just how expensive a typographical error can be after he signed and mailed a letter informing a prospective client that he would charge a "fat fee" (instead of a "flat fee").

All misspellings and mistypings are the responsibility of the author, not of the typist. If you cannot replace an incompetent typist, learn to proofread your own work with extra care. If you have difficulty spelling correctly, keep a list of words that you regularly misspell in your line of vision when you write and have someone who spells correctly proofread your work.

CHAPTER 7

THE TOTAL PRODUCT: APPELLATE BRIEFS AND ARGUMENTATIVE MEMORANDA

§ 7.1 INTRODUCTION

This chapter explains special features of briefs, described generally in Chapter 1, and suggests techniques for presenting these features in a persuasive style. Then it discusses techniques for writing persuasive arguments. The basis for discussion will be a brief for an appellate court. The suggestions also apply to argumentative briefs and memoranda prepared for trial and administrative judges, although the form, permissible length, and degree of formality may differ at those levels of argument.

Brief writing is formal. The content, the format, the wording, and the writer's tone are all subject to conventions, discussed below. Appellate court rules provide detailed requirements for page size, length, necessary subdivisions, order of subdivisions, general content, and covers (even the color may be prescribed). The Rules on Appeal of the United States Supreme Court (those effective June 30, 1980) are cited as the basis for many suggestions in this section. These rules are representative of other courts' requirements for appeal briefs as well. Remember, however, to consult the controlling rules before beginning to write any brief or argumentative memorandum.

§ 7.2 PREPARATION FOR WRITING

Preparation will begin with a review of the record of the case and of prior research on the legal issues. Tentative decisions must be made as to which facts in the record are significant and which legal arguments to use. Then the Argument section of the brief may be tentatively outlined, perhaps in the form of the logical series of contentions. Finally, decisions can be made about questions to be stated. After tentative identification of the questions, the record may be reviewed again one or more times before firm decisions are made about the questions and arguments to be presented.

A limited number of questions and arguments should be selected. In general, judges and other specialists on appellate advocacy agree that argument on numerous questions may detract from rather than enhance overall persuasiveness. Common advice is to argue the strongest points—perhaps only two or three—even though there are many attractive possibilities. These specialists suggest that if you cannot win on the strong-

est points, you should not expect to win on the
weaker points; argument on many points may only annoy the judges. Of course, a case may be so
complex that many questions must be argued, for
example, if reversal can be justified only by
favorable answers to numerous questions. Even
in a complex case, however, questions can be related to each other and combined so as to reduce
the number of questions formally stated as
"Questions Presented." The following guidelines
should help you to select the questions to argue:

(i)   Prefer the strong points over the weak
      points.

(ii) Other things being equal,

      a.   prefer simple questions over complex
           questions, and

      b.   prefer related questions over unrelat-
           ed questions.

The order of the discussion in the following sections should not be regarded as the necessary order for writing a brief. Where one begins in
writing a brief depends on the individual and the
nature of the case. The following discussion begins with the Questions Presented only because
they appear first in Supreme Court brief form.
The order of the remaining discussion also follows the Supreme Court's form.

§ 7.3 WRITING EFFECTIVE QUESTIONS

From the viewpoint of judges, the function of questions is to provide a quick picture of a case about which they know nothing. Questions must be written to serve that function. From the viewpoint of counsel, an additional function of questions is to provide the judges with a favorable picture of a case. Questions should therefore be written to serve that persuasive function—but without misleading or alienating the judges. That calls for skill and the touch of an artist.

The quick-picture function of questions is emphasized by the recently revised rules of the United States Supreme Court that place the Questions Presented first: before the Table of Contents, before the Statement of the Case, before the ten other subdivisions required in a brief or in a petition for writ of certiorari (discretionary review) or in a jurisdictional statement (appeal as of right). Some other courts' rules also require that questions (or points or assignments of error) appear as one of the early subdivisions. Therefore, just as in a memorandum, the questions must be meaningful standing alone.

The Supreme Court rules describe questions that are effective from the justices' viewpoint: "The questions presented shall be expressed in the terms and circumstances of the case but without unnecessary detail. The statement of the questions should be short and concise and should not be argumentative or repetitious." Rule 15.-1(a), 21.1(a), and 34.1(a). The description provides useful guidelines for all questions. The need to state questions in "terms and circumstances" of a case (that is, to incorporate key facts) rather than in abstract terms has been emphasized in Chapter 6 in the description of effective questions for memoranda. To say that questions should be "short and concise" and not "repetitious" is to state a fundamental rule of writing. That the questions should not be "argumentative," however, may seem to conflict with counsel's goal to state questions that will persuade the judges to accept the counsel's viewpoint. Questions can be drafted to be persuasive, however, without being argumentative.

To write a persuasive question, you must state a question on which the outcome of the case depends and ask it in such a way that only one reasonable answer follows: yours. The facts to be included must be selected carefully for their persuasive value. The sentence itself must be rhetorically structured so as to emphasize the most favorable facts. The conclusion that the court is to reach should be implicit. All this must be done without distorting either the law or the facts and without appearing to be argumentative. Here are examples of effective questions written from opposing viewpoints.

Petitioner's question: Does Title VII of the Civil Rights Act of 1964 make unlawful a program, adopted by an employer and a union in collective bargaining, which reserves for black bidders 50% of the openings in an in-plant training program in order to eliminate a racial imbalance in the skilled craft workforce?

Respondent's question: Whether under Title VII of the Civil Rights Act of 1964 an employer and a labor union may, solely in order to achieve a desired ratio of minority workers in craft positions at a manufacturing plant, institute a racial quota for admission to craft training programs in the absence of any prior discrimination against the minority workers at that plant.

Here, on the other hand, is a question that is argumentative.

Whether under Title VII of the Civil Rights Act of 1964 an employer and a labor union may institute a racial quota for admission to training programs that is preferential to recently hired members of minority groups and discriminates against whites, who are thus deprived of rights to entry into training programs earned under job seniority acquired through years of labor.

Another ineffective type of question is the conclusory question, one that states the nature of the conclusion to be reached without giving a clue about the specific answer, for example, "The question is whether the complaint is legally insufficient." The desired conclusion should be implic-

it in the question, for example: "Is a complaint
for breach of contract insufficient in law if it does
not allege performance by the plaintiff or offer
any excuse for her nonperformance?"

Questions Presented may be stated in either
question form or declarative form ("The question
is . . ." or "Whether . . .").

§ 7.4 WRITING THE STATEMENT OF THE CASE

(a) The Nature of the Case

The Statement of the Case consists primarily of
a statement of the significant facts of the case.
First, however, the legal scene must be set with a
description of the nature of the proceeding if that
is not stated before or as a part of the Questions
Presented. The description should be a short
paragraph that identifies the general subject of
the case and how it was disposed of in the lower
court.

> This is an action for damages for interference
> with an alleged contractual relationship. After trial
> before the court without a jury, judgment was en-
> tered against the defendants for $127,000.

A summary of additional procedural details may
be necessary, but try to avoid a lengthy summary
of procedural steps before the human side of the
case is introduced. For example, first identify
the parties (if your client might evoke a sympa-

thetic attitude) or interweave the review of necessary procedural details with the narration of facts. (The governing rules may, however, require a separate summary of the pleadings and procedure.) Summarize only those procedural steps that are material to the questions to be argued or necessary to an understanding of the case.

(b) The Statement of Facts

How the facts are stated may be more important than the argument of law itself. Judges frequently advise lawyers to spend more time on facts and less time on legal arguments. The judges initially know nothing about the case. They want to know what happened, when, where, and to whom. Do not deaden this desire to know with an overly detailed or dry recital.

The facts must be candidly set forth, but the writer may arrange them, phrase them, and expand or condense treatment of particular events so as to emphasize favorable facts and to diminish unfavorable facts. Juxtaposition, placement within sentences and paragraphs, choice of verbs and nouns: all of these assist in presenting facts in a persuasive way.

Careful selection is the first step toward writing a persuasive fact statement. Both favorable and unfavorable facts must be included. Disputed and undisputed facts and alleged and established facts must be distinguished in order to establish the writer's credibility or ethical appeal. Only material facts should be included with the possible exception of substantively non-material details that add human interest or create the desired impression or context. Use of non-material details for this purpose, however, must be limited and subtle. Visual details and direct conversation may be used to arouse the reader's interest and draw the reader into the event. Selection of all these kinds of human interest details should be carefully limited, however, to avoid unduly extending the statement of facts.

Careful arrangement is the second step toward a persuasive fact statement. Use a simple organizational pattern. Remember that the judges are not familiar with the facts. The judges will assimilate the facts more readily if they are stated in chronological order or in clearly defined topical order. If the fact statement is long, use headings to help the reader understand, relate, and remember the facts.

Careful presentation of facts is the third step toward a persuasive fact summary. The following suggestions should help you to set forth the facts clearly and favorably without distorting them.

Refer to parties as descriptively as possible. For example, use "husband" and "wife" in a domestic relations case; use "employer" and "employee" (or "worker") in a labor dispute; use "plaintiff" and "defendant" in a negligence case. Select designations that will be readily understood and remembered. Give special attention to distinctive designations in a case involving many parties. In such complex litigation, use of the parties' names may promote clarity once relationships have been stated. Use of the parties' formal titles (for example, Appellant) should be kept to a minimum once the parties have been identified.

Do not hide unfavorable facts, but do not highlight them either. For example, place such facts between prior and subsequent statements of related favorable facts. Conclude with a fact or event favorable to your client's position, not with an unfavorable fact.

Use short sentences to increase readability. Use forceful verbs and nouns, chosen to characterize your client advantageously and to depict events favorably, but not so forceful that a fair-minded reader will lose faith in your credibility. Cases in which one party is always fair and right and the other party is always mean and wrong are a rarity. Use adjectives sparingly and selectively; avoid adjectives that reflect bias, such as "reactionary" or "hysterical."

Avoid an obtrusive style: let the facts speak for themselves. Do not argue or editorialize. Instead, rely on selection, juxtaposition, and careful word choice for persuasion.

Use diagrams or charts to present complicated facts, relationships, or chronology of events.

After writing the Argument section, review the fact statement. Add any significant facts that were omitted in the first draft; omit any unnecessary facts that were included. Be certain that you have supported fact statements by accurate references to the record in the form required by governing rules.

§ 7.5 WRITING EFFECTIVE POINT HEADINGS

A point heading is a concise, persuasive statement of a conclusion or reason that you want the court to accept. Point headings are used as the headings and subheadings within the Argument section of a brief. They are also included in the Table of Contents of the brief to provide a concise summary of the parts of the argument. Point headings should therefore be written both to persuade and to summarize.

First identify the conclusions that a court must accept in order to decide in your client's favor, and identify reasons that support those conclusions. The general conclusions will be answers

[*174*]

to the Questions Presented, but you will also want to identify other specific conclusions that are necessary to acceptance of your client's position.

Then outline the necessary conclusions. Decide on an order that will, if logically possible, put your strongest points (arguments) at the beginning. Use an order that keeps related parts of the argument together.

Once you have decided on the subject matter and order, write the point headings, using persuasive sentence structure and language. Keep in mind the following generally accepted guidelines for effective point headings.

Use full sentences, not topical phrases.

Unacceptable topical heading:

The alleged contractual relationship.

Use statements about your case, not abstract legal principles.

Unacceptable abstract heading:

A third party is liable for interference with contractual relations only if there is an interference with a valid contractual relationship or business expectancy.

Use statements that demonstrate legal relevance.

Legal relevance not demonstrated:

Plaintiff's evidence failed to establish a valid contractual relationship or business expectancy.

Finally, avoid long, complex statements.

Here is a point heading that demonstrates effective use of these guidelines:

> Plaintiff has not proved that Defendant tortiously interfered with his exchange contract because Plaintiff's evidence failed to establish the existence of a valid contractual relationship of the type entitled to protection against interference by third parties.

Notice that the foregoing point heading incorporates both the conclusion and the supporting reason. A point heading may also state only a conclusion or a reason. Subpoint headings may then supply the supporting reason for a conclusion or the conclusions to be drawn from a reason.

With the above guidelines in mind, compare the following three sets of point headings taken from briefs filed before the United States Supreme Court in *United Steelworkers of America v. Weber*, 443 U.S. 193 (1979). Note departures from the guidelines suggested above. Do such lapses influence your understanding of the nature of the case?

From Brief for Petitioner-Union:

I. THE KAISER–USWA SELECTION PROGRAM DOES NOT VIOLATE TITLE VII

    A. The Statutory Language

    B. The 1964 Legislative History

        1. The Genesis of the House Bill

        2. The Judiciary Committee Report

3. The House Floor Debate

4. The Senate

5. House Consideration of the Senate Amendments

6. The Interplay Between Title IV and Title VII

    a. The Decision under Title IV

    b. The Link to Title VII

C. The Meaning of the 1964 Legislative History

D. The 1972 Legislative History

II. ALTERNATIVE THEORIES PREMISED UPON ASSUMED GOVERNMENTAL POWERS ARE NOT APPROPRIATE BASES FOR DECIDING THIS CASE

III. FINAL CONSIDERATIONS

From Brief for the United States and the Equal Employment Opportunity Commission:

The Gramercy training programs are a permissible form of voluntary affirmative action under Title VII

A. Title VII permits, and often requires, employers to take race-conscious action

B. Devising remedies for discrimination may require consideration of race

    1. The legislative history of the 1964 Act

    2. The legislative history of the 1972 amendments to Title VII

C. Title VII permits private parties to take affirmative action to remedy apparent employment discrimination similar to the relief

[*177*]

that a court could order to remedy proven discrimination

D. Kaiser could reasonably believe it would be found liable for discriminating against blacks at the Gramercy plant

E. The Gramercy training programs were appropriate remedies for the apparent Title VII violations in hiring for the craft positions

F. Title VII authorizes employers to take affirmative action in response to Executive Order 11246

    1. The Executive Order program requires government contractors to take affirmative action, without need for proof of prior discrimination by each contractor

    2. The Executive Order program is consistent with Title VII

    3. The Gramercy training programs were consistent with the Executive Order program

From an amicus brief:

I. Title VII Does Not Prohibit an Employer and a Union from Adopting Reasonable Race Conscious Measures to Overcome the Absence of Minorities from Skilled Jobs

II. The Kaiser-Steelworker Training Agreement is Lawful Under Title VII

A. The Record Establishes a Basis for Remedial Action

B. The Training Program was a Reasonable Response to the Absence of Blacks in Craft Jobs

§ 7.6 WRITING AN EFFECTIVE SUMMARY OF THE ARGUMENT

Although the summary of the argument is placed before the argument in a brief, it should be written after the argument has been both written and revised. It answers the questions presented as succinctly as possible while outlining the reasoning that supports the answers.

The Supreme Court, in Rule 34.1(h), recommends: "The summary should be a suitably paragraphed . . . succinct, but accurate and clear, condensation of the argument actually made in the body of the brief. It should not be a mere repetition of the headings under which the argument is arranged."

The summary should be more than a mere assertion of your client's right to win the case. It should present the crux of the argument. It should weave together the strands of argument from the brief and identify the logical relationships between key points. Normally no authorities are discussed, although citations to one or two crucial cases may be included.

The paragraphs of the summary are set off with numerals or letters corresponding to divisions of the argument proper.

§ 7.7 WRITING THE CONCLUSION

A conclusion "specifying with particularity" the relief requested is required by the United States Supreme Court rule. Some counsel believe that if arguments have been persuasively and cohesively presented, nothing more is required. Other counsel believe that the basic arguments should also be briefly summarized. If such a summary is included, it should be extremely brief. The requested relief should be specified first for the benefit of any judge who might regard a summary as unnecessary repetition. The basic arguments may then be succinctly presented as reasons for granting the requested relief. The relationship between multiple arguments should be identified, as in the following brief conclusion.

> The judgment for plaintiff should be reversed. Plaintiff did not have a valid contract or a business expectancy of the type protected against tortious interference. In the alternative, the conduct of defendant, as a competitor, was privileged.

§ 7.8 THE ARGUMENT: WRITING TO PERSUADE

(a) General Writing Goals

Test your readiness to draft any argument by trying to state in one sentence the conclusion that you want the court to reach. Then attempt to change places with the judges. Ask yourself what you would want to know first if you sat in a judge's chair. How would you want the law presented? As you draft, keep in mind a judge who may be tired, who may be reading your brief after reading others on different subjects, or who may be able to devote only limited time to considering it. Structure your brief from its beginning to its conclusion so that the judges will be able to scan it rapidly and understand your case and your argument quickly. Judges are not always able to study each brief in detail.

Following are other general writing goals to keep in mind while drafting an argument.

Get to the point. Explain what your client wants and why. Tell the court what you want in the first page or two of the brief, not in the middle or at the end. Explain exactly what you want the court to do.

Give the best argument first. Tell the court first the best reason for deciding in your favor. One point—simply, directly, and persuasively argued—is sometimes all you need.

Keep your argument simple. Your case should make sense to the court in terms of everyday life. It should show the court how the people involved may be handled fairly and humanely within the structure of the law.

Be concise. Judges universally complain that briefs are too long. They complain that there is too much laborious, unapplied case analysis and too little effort to revise and condense. From the judge's point of view, shorter is better.

Remember that string citations and multiple cases are rarely helpful and that long quotations from cases and other authorities may not be read.

(b) Controlling Tone

Tone is often overlooked by legal writers. It is never overlooked by readers. Any conspicuous tone interferes with reception of content by causing the reader to react first to the tone and only secondly to the subject matter. That is true whether the tone is informal, stuffy, pretentious, hyperbolic, bitter, casual, or uncertain.

Tone must be carefully controlled in brief writing, for judges may begin to react favorably or unfavorably to the substance of an argument according to the way its tone affects them. This is often a subconscious reaction, making it nearly impossible for the reader to make allowance for an irritating tone.

The following fact statement from a brief submitted for the Petitioner in a recent case demonstrates uncontrolled tone:

A couple of weeks thereafter, while in flight from crime, he again tried to do himself in in a Reno hotel.

Furthermore, before entering his guilty plea, he kept
on slashing at himself and eating light bulbs. The
ingestion of light bulbs also causes doubt as to Petitioner's ability to aid his Counsel.

The tone varies from stuffy ("thereafter," "flight
from crime," "ingestion causes doubt") to colloquial ("a couple of," "do himself in," "kept on"),
making the fact statement ludicrous. Because
the tone is out of control, the court may have difficulty according credibility to the writer.

The following guidelines can help you control
the tone of your briefs.

Establish an assertive or emphatic tone by
making direct, not indirect, assertions. (Indirect
assertions: "It appears to be the case that," "It
can be argued," "It was clear to the court that,"
"It is conceivable that," "One feature of which
one should be aware.") Do not, however, be ag-
gressive. Do not tell the court what it must do
or think. The court will decide for itself what is
or is not persuasive authority.

Beware of humor unless you know your audience well. Attempted humor may annoy one or
more judges of a court. However, judges, like all
readers, appreciate the lightening, sometimes en-
lightening, effect of figures of speech, examples,
and famous sayings—used sparingly.

Here is an example of humor that works because it grows directly out of the subject matter (legality of a search of defendant's person):

> When Officer Shallow patted down the Defendant, he discovered nothing but two lobster tails. Officer Shallow testified that he immediately recognized them as lobster tails and immediately knew that they were not weapons. Yet the search did not end with this discovery . . . .. Lobster tails are not contraband; there is no law against carrying concealed lobster tails with or without a sales receipt. Lobster tails are not inherently suspect. Nor do they become suspect because they are frozen or because they bear the label of the store that packaged them.

Do not make the case sound ridiculously easy or opposing counsel sound ridiculously blind. An arrogant or superior tone will not advance your case. For example, a sentence such as, "Cases cited by Plaintiff are inapposite and easily distinguishable," may offend or annoy the judicial reader who finds the plaintiff's cases difficult to distinguish. Similarly, a court may form a negative opinion of a writer who facetiously uses the pronoun "one" to attack opposing counsel. "One is really at a loss to see how this argument can even be made" or "A reading of Plaintiff's Memorandum to the Court leaves one with a certain sense of confusion." Sarcasm is never appropriate. Neither is an insulting or intemperate tone, however much opposing counsel deserves it.

Avoid informality, especially as expressed in colloquialism, for example, "Whoever would have thought that Mr. Butler would go and shoot him!" Colloquial terms or phrases, as in this extreme example, are imprecise by nature; they have no fixed meanings (which explains why we rely on them in conversation). Informal abbreviations like "ad," "auto," "cite," "exam," "gas," "memo," "phone," and "quote" are also inappropriate. On the other hand, avoid excessive formality. Stuffiness, as much as chumminess, distracts the reader from your ideas.

Use "we" for yourself and your client, and use "counsel for appellant or respondent" for opposing counsel. Do not use "you" to refer to the court. Do not use "I" to refer to yourself.

(c) Using Rhetorical Devices for Persuasion

Rhetorical devices are means of achieving emphasis through special sentence structure, paragraph design, and wording. Many of these devices are explained elsewhere in this *Nutshell*. The most effective devices are illustrated in this subsection.

The key to effective use of any rhetorical device is subtlety: the device must appear natural. It must not attract attention as a gimmick being used on the reader. The exception is the appeal to logic. That rhetorical appeal is more effective if it is obvious.   Appeals to emotion, in contrast, will fail if obvious.

(1) Achieving Emphasis With Sentence Structures

A. Place stressed words at the beginning and at the end of sentences.   Use short sentences for special emphasis as in the following example.

> Whether surveillance is electronic, optical, or human is irrelevant where there is no reasonable expectation of privacy.   While on a public street, the defendant had no such reasonable expectation.

In a conspicuous position, understatement is more effective than overstatement.   The above example would be less effective if the words "clearly," "certainly," or "obviously" were added ("the defendant *obviously* had no such reasonable expectation").

B. Avoid beginning a sentence with an equivocation, such as, "it would seem to be" or "it may be that."   Instead, write forcefully "it must follow that," or simply begin with the point itself and then state necessary qualifications.

C. Put subordinate thoughts in less emphatic positions.   Compare this pair of sentences:

> The result is that enforcement of the rescission right is not uniform among the circuit courts.   (The phrase "among circuit courts" receives undue emphasis.)

The result is that enforcement of the rescission right among the circuit courts *is not uniform.* (The important words "result" and "is not uniform" receive the emphasis they deserve.)

D. Use active voice for forcefulness.

See discussion of active and passive voice in Chapter 4.

E. Make affirmative assertions. Even negative ideas can be expressed in positive, therefore more forceful, form.

The approach of the English courts is somewhat uncertain and less clear-cut than that of the American courts.

Revised: The approach of the American courts is more clearly defined than that of the English courts.

F. Use double negatives sparingly for understatement. The double negative, such as "not infrequently," has a respectable history as a rhetorical device for emphasis. Although it has fallen out of favor, it may still be employed on occasion as a means of understatement. For example, "not wholly unsuccessful" understates a lack of success, thus emphasizing it, as compared to its affirmative form "partially successful," which emphasizes a degree of success.

G. Use parallel constructions to draw attention to similar ideas.

In *Cooper* the court considered damage to a number of motor cars caused by the negligence of a painting contractor. In *Runnels* the court considered damage to construction machinery caused by the negligence of the mechanic who repaired it.

H. Use parallel constructions for rhetorical effect. Similarity of structure in a pair or series of related words, phrases, or clauses will make them more memorable. ("He tried to make the law clear, precise, and equitable.") The principle of parallelism is that like things be phrased in like terms.

Varieties of parallelism include:

Repetition of the same word or group of words at the beginning of successive clauses (anaphora): "They were common, though prohibited by law. They were common, though condemned by public opinion." This scheme establishes rhythm and produces a strong emotional effect.

Repetition of the same word or group of words at the ends of successive clauses (epistrophe): "To the good American many subjects are sacred: Children are sacred, business is sacred, property is sacred." This scheme sets up a pronounced rhythm and special emphasis by repetition of words and by putting words in the emphatic final position.

Repetition of last word of one clause at the beginning of the following clause (anadiplosis): "The crime was common; common be the pain."

Repetition of words, in successive clauses, in reverse grammatical order (antimetabole): "One should work to live, not live to work." Antimetabole gives the air of the neatly turned phrase.

Juxtaposition of contrasting ideas, often in parallel structure (antithesis): "Though argumentative, he was modest." The opposition in an antithesis can reside either in words or in ideas, or both.

I. Rhetorical questions, that is, questions to which no immediate reply is expected, may be used sparingly as emphatic variations of affirmative statements.

Did Mr. Bertleson have a right to use his easement in accordance with the express language of his covenant?

(2) Achieving Emphasis With Paragraphing

A. Use persuasive paragraph structure. In each section of a brief or in each paragraph, state your argument or position first—not your opponent's—and state it affirmatively. Then dispense with your opponent's argument. To make paragraphs affirmative: (i) State your argument or position first. (ii) Acknowledge contrary evidence, or state the opposing argument in the middle of the paragraph. (iii) Refute contrary evidence or opposing argument. (iv) Restate your argument as a conclusion.

One purpose of this structure is to put favorable arguments and facts in the most conspicuous place (the beginning and the end). The interior of a paragraph should contain less important elements. Both unfavorable facts and arguments must be included, of course, but they will be given less emphasis in the middle of a paragraph.

Another purpose of this structure is to give a balanced analysis of the issue, that is, to reflect fair consideration of both sides even if only one is fully developed in the paragraph.

Example of an unpersuasive paragraph structure:

Warwick v. Woodinville Company, 100 Wash. 200, 174 P. 15 (1920), however, represents an archaic view of "publication," and it may not be binding precedent today. More recent cases adopt the rule that to establish defamation when information is circulated among those with a "common interest" requires a showing of malice or bad faith. Applied here, if false medical information were circulated among supervisors evaluating an employee, a common interest in the information would probably be established. The complaining party would be required to show that the false statement was made with malice or in bad faith. *See, e.g., Sam v. Painter's Local Union*, 40 Wn.2d 800, 200 P.2d 754 (1955). Even though false medical information was circulated among Company personnel, who see the material in the course of their normal duties, the lack of evidence of bad faith distinguishes this case from *Warwick*.

In the above example, both unfavorable authority and an unfavorable fact appear in positions of emphasis. Recent authority and the present requirements for establishing defamation should be emphasized instead, as in the following revision.

> *Revised*: Plaintiff has presented no evidence of malice or bad faith and therefore has not established that defamatory statements were made. A showing of malice or bad faith is necessary to establish defamation when allegedly false information is circulated among persons with a "common interest." See *e.g., Sam v. Painter's Local Union,* 40 Wn.2d 800, 200 P. 2d 754 (1955). Such "common interest" can be found in Defendant's circulation of medical information among supervisors evaluating an employee because the supervisors see the information in the course of their normal duties. Plaintiff's primary case, *Warwick v. Woodinville Company,* 100 Wash. 200, 174 P. 15 (1920), was decided before the court required evidence of malice or bad faith under these circumstances. Having failed to present evidence of malice or bad faith, Plaintiff has not satisfied present requirements for establishing defamation.

B. Use short paragraphs for emphasis. A short paragraph, like a short, climactic sentence, provides emphasis automatically. A one-sentence paragraph will provide extra emphasis, but only if used sparingly and skillfully. The following example illustrates effective use of a one-sentence paragraph.

> Plaintiff's brief does not refer to the Plan itself. Rather, plaintiff ignores the legal text and argues on the basis of a summary description of the Plan

contained in a booklet, "Company Employee Retirement Plan." The booklet states that it is a summary and that "for a proper understanding of the Plan, the complete text should be read."

Construction of the Plan is controlled by its legal text and not by selective citations from a summary booklet.

(3) Achieving Emphasis With Language

"Now, words in their proper order are the raw material of the law, and words have a magic of their own; they have color and sound and meaning and associations. But choice words in the right order have a more magical power still." —Birkett, *Law and Literature: The Equipment of the Lawyer,* 36 A.B. A.J. 891, 946 (1950) (Excerpted with permission from the American Bar Association Journal.)

A. Remember to consider word connotation. Words create impressions. The writer's task is to choose words that create the appropriate impressions for his or her persuasive purpose. While writing each word, keep your objective in mind: For example, are you trying to establish guilt, liability, a violation of constitutional rights?

Nouns: Nouns have negative or positive connotations; use them carefully and purposefully.

Positive	Negative
offense	crime
offender	criminal
control	coercion
debate	argument
reconstruction	fabrication

eminence	notoriety
adversary	enemy
rapid disassembly	explosion

Verbs: Verbs provide the most subtle, thus the most effective, coloration. Statements may be "affirmed" (implies trust), "asserted" (neutral), or "alleged" (implies doubt). The verb "sever," for example, makes a stronger impression than the verbs "cut" and "break."

Use active verbs, such as "conceal," "ignore," and "intend" rather than forms of the weak verb "to be" or its substitutes, "seem," "become," "exist," "appear," "arise," "relate to," "deal with," "involve," and "concern."

Adjectives: Use a minimum of these because they are less subtle than either nouns or verbs. Do not pile up similar adjectives like "inequitable and unconscionable." If an adjective is necessary, use only one and choose it carefully. As Voltaire remarked, the adjective is the enemy of the noun.

B. Use ornamental language cautiously. While neither lawyers nor their clients are willing to pay for literary skill for its own sake, one mark of an expert legal writer is the ability to use vivid examples, interesting similes, metaphors, or analogies. This ability grows out of a sensitivity to language, to how it sounds, and to what auditory and visual effects it has on the reader. It grows out of an awareness of human nature. Prose that delights us also instructs us more efficiently and effectively than writing that deadens our senses.

The ability to use figurative language skillfully develops over a lifetime of writing. The ability may, however, be cultivated by paying attention to the sensory dimension of words. Metaphors and similes should be fresh. Do not mix metaphors, for example, "We need this case like a horse needs a fifth wheel"; "when we come to that bridge, we will swim over it"; "they smelled a rat and nipped it in the bud"; or "they built their argument on fuzzy ground." Clichés should be avoided unless "renovated" (for example, "no truer words were ever silenced").

C. Avoid unpersuasive wording. Many words and phrases actually impair the persuasiveness of a piece of writing. Carefully avoid all the following bad habits:

Avoid overuse of "clear" and "clearly" in a brief. These do not persuade the court that the case is clearly in your favor or even clear at all. These overused words may irritate the judicial reader. "Obvious" and "obviously" are similarly objectionable.

Avoid expressions of supposed candor, modesty, or any other attempts at personal expression. Some of the worst examples are: "frankly," "to be frank," "to be honest," "with all candor," "candidly," "I humbly disagree," "I do not pretend to be an expert."

Do not use words sarcastically or ironically to mean something other than their dictionary meaning. For example, in this sentence taken from a state supreme court brief, the word "remarkable" might boomerang on its author if the court agrees with the contention:

> Plaintiffs make the remarkable contention that the "well-established doctrine of restraint" is the appropriate rule.

Avoid words made trite by overuse. Both psychological terms and computer jargon have become trite and have a negative effect on many readers. The following words, among many others, have been degraded by imprecise use and overuse: actualize, appropriate, definitive, effectuate, duplicative, exacerbate, finalize, functional, impact, implement (as verb), interaction, interface, input, meaningful dialogue, ongoing, optimize, qualitative, quantitative, quality (as adjective), relevant criteria, replicate, supportive, synchronization, tension, thrust (as noun), update (as noun or verb), viable.

(4) *Using Classical Devices for Persuasion*

The devices for persuasion have not changed since they were studied and described by the

Greeks.   Three of the more important of these devices are discussed below.

A. Logical Appeal.   Although the emotional and ethical appeal should never be ignored, the logical appeal is the most important and persuasive for the advocate.   The logical appeal in legal writing is chiefly an appeal to precedent.   Like cases are logically decided alike.   The writer's task is to demonstrate the similarity or dissimilarity of decided cases with the client's case.

B. Emotional and Ethical Appeals.   Remember that argumentative writing affects a reader's emotions and conveys an image of the author. Too often law students and lawyers aim only at a reader's logical mind and forget to consider the reader's emotions.   After you have identified the result you want, identify the emotion or combination of emotions that will lead the reader to that result.   Then select the details of your case that will arouse that emotion: these should be subtly emphasized in your argument.

Any writer is more persuasive if the reader respects her or him.   This respect, traditionally called the ethical appeal, emerges from what is written as well as from how it is written.   An image of honesty and straightforwardness should emerge, beginning with the fact statement.   The writer should set forth the facts and all that follows in a well balanced and reasonable way.   The writer must not appear to be blinded by emotion. Nor should the writer be timid or apologetic. The best image for a brief writer is that of a strong but reasonable counselor, unafraid of taking a stand but not willing to exaggerate or contort the facts or law to make a point.

Brief-writers inevitably find weak spots in their own cases. A good rule of thumb is to be critical of your case before the reader is. Acknowledge and then overcome obvious weaknesses through authority, policy, or reason; account for weaknesses in your case before your reader discovers them. You will thus create an image of objectivity, while simultaneously making an appeal to the reason and logic of your reader.

Sophisticated brief-writers sometimes make educated allusions to historical events or people or repeat famous aphorisms in order to convey an image of urbanity and broadmindedness. A novice should avoid such flourishes; they are the prerogative of experienced lawyers and judges. It is enough to establish an image of reasonableness by reflecting your understanding of both sides of a case, by conceding small points when necessary, and by acknowledging the possible validity of the opposing argument while undercutting it.

(5) Avoiding Ineffective Emphasis

Mechanical contrivances like italics, underlining, boldface type, dashes, and exclamation marks should not normally be used for emphasis. (For appropriate use of italics, dashes, and exclamation marks, see Chapter 8.) In typewritten text, underlining does provide a clear visual signal to the reader. Thus, underlining may be useful in certain writing situations, always provided that it is used carefully and sparingly, not indiscriminately.

§ 7.9 THE FINAL TOUCH

Careful revision is essential. Do not permit your focus on persuasive writing to overshadow other important techniques and details of writing. See Section 6.4.

CHAPTER 8

PUNCTUATION, GRAMMAR, AND MECHANICS

§ 8.1 INTRODUCTION

Legal writers must have full command of punctuation, grammar, and mechanics. Punctuation tells the reader how to read a sentence or paragraph. Thus, the legal writer must punctuate precisely in order to control meaning. This "tight" punctuation requires a better understanding of the basic rules than many undergraduates have before they enter law school. "Loose" punctuation, punctuation that yields more than one interpretation, is permitted and sometimes encouraged in undergraduate writing courses. The legal writer, however, should never punctuate loosely. Doing so creates the risk of misreading by a judge, another lawyer, or a client.

The punctuation section in this chapter covers those rules most commonly violated by law students and lawyers. The rules receiving greatest emphasis are those that prevent ambiguity and that save the reader from having to reread for comprehension.

Grammar refers to syntax, that is, to sentence structure. As young children we learn to speak grammatically. If we did not, no one would understand us. An ungrammatical "sentence" might be: "Documented doubtful the was fully claim." We know, as English speakers, how to make that grammatical. Without much effort, we can arrange it meaningfully in several ways, all determined by the grammar of our language: "The doubtful claim was fully documented." "Fully documented was the doubtful claim." "The doubtful claim was documented fully." Grammar also refers to the "operating principles" of our language, for example, correct use of inflections and parts of speech. It is ungrammatical to say "I do not know *who* you mean" (rather than *whom*) or "The letter was signed by him and *I*" (rather than *me*). For most native speakers, grammar is instinctive and understandable. However, if a child learns to speak ungrammatically in a particular way, and if that child's schooling does not correct the error, then as an adult speaker and writer, he or she may have an ungrammatical habit. The section below on grammar is intended to point out the most common of these ungrammatical habits.

Mechanics, as used in this chapter, refers simply to manuscript form. The correct uses of italics, ellipsis points, typographical conventions, and ·

a few other technical devices are briefly covered below.

§ 8.2 PUNCTUATION

(a) Introduction

In legal writing, there are no significant variations from standard usage. While writing, use a standard grammar or usage handbook as a desk reference. If you are unable to find a solution to a punctuation problem in this *Nutshell* or in your handbook, at least punctuate consistently in the same piece of writing.

(b) Use of the Comma

(1) Use a Compound Sentence Comma for Clarity

Use a comma to separate two independent clauses joined by "and," "but," "or," "for," "nor," or "yet." The comma precedes the conjunction.

Confusing: The plaintiff's car hit the newsstand and the defendant failed to stop. (The reader may at first think that the car hit the newsstand and the defendant. The appearance of "failed" sends the reader back to re-read the sentence.)

Clear: The plaintiff's car hit the newsstand, and the defendant failed to stop. (The comma signals a completed unit of thought. The reader is then prepared for a new subject in a new clause.)

(2) Do Not Use a Comma With Compound Subjects, Verbs, and Objects

Legal writers use interior coordination frequently; that is, they use compound subjects, verbs, and objects, joined by coordinating conjunctions. These are often mispunctuated, as in the following examples.

1. *Incorrect division of a compound verb*: The Trust Fund suspended payments to plaintiff effective April 1980, and further determined that contributions received on his behalf should be refunded.

Corrected: The Trust Fund suspended payments to plaintiff effective April 1980 and further determined that contributions received on his behalf should be refunded.

2. *Incorrect division of a compound object*: The appellants contend that the facts alleged by appellants in their answer were not sufficient to constitute duress, and that the case was controlled by *Ingebrigt v. Seattle Taxicab & Transfer Co.*

Corrected: The appellants contend that the facts alleged by appellants in their answer were not sufficient to constitute duress and that the case was controlled by *Ingebrigt v. Seattle Taxicab & Transfer Co.*

3. *Incorrect division of a compound subject*: No compensation for performing services for another, or wages appear on the employer's records.

Corrected: No wages or compensation for performing services for another appears on the employer's records. (Note that the verb "appears" agrees with the closer subject "compensation" because one of the subjects joined by "or" is plural and the other is singular.)

(3) Use Two Commas to Set Off Interruptions

Commas are used to enclose parenthetical, explanatory, or interruptive words, phrases, or clauses. These commas mark the boundaries of a phrase or clause. Thus, use two unless one is replaced by a period or other mark of punctuation.

1. A lawyer, with a stroke of the pen, can save an estate from the IRS.

2. The plaintiff's car hit the utility pole, according to witnesses, and thus caused a three-hour power outage.

3. Will you help us, at your convenience, by providing the policy number?

(4) Use Commas for Nonrestrictive Phrases or Clauses

One essential use of the interrupting comma is to indicate nonrestriction, that is, a commenting word, phrase, or clause. Conversely, the absence of an interrupting comma indicates restriction, that is, a limiting word, phrase, or clause. For example, the interrupting commas in the following example tells us that there is only one defendant, not several: "The defendant, the Jordan

Company, requests dismissal of the charge." If
there were more than one defendant, the commas
would be omitted: "Defendant Jordan Company
requests dismissal of the charge."

A simple way to illustrate the difference between restriction and nonrestriction is by limiting
or not limiting a category:

Category: tort

Restriction: a tort that involves a breach of contract (or, a tort that does not involve a breach of contract)

Nonrestriction (explanatory, not limiting): a tort,
which ordinarily falls within the domain of civil action, ...

(5) Use a Comma With "Which" But Not With "That"

The use of "that" signals a limiting function;
in other words, it introduces a restriction of the
preceding word or phrase.

Restrictive: The judges will read the briefs that
are well written.   (Only the well-written briefs will
be read.)

The use of "which" signals a non-defining function; in other words, it does not restrict the preceding word or phrase.

Nonrestrictive: The judges will read the briefs,
which are well written.   (All the briefs will be read;
all the briefs are well written.)

Since many writers use "which" for both defining and non-defining clauses, a comma must be
used to make the distinction clear. A comma preceding a "which" clause signals a non-defining
function. Absence of a comma signals that the
clause is defining.

(6) Do Not Use a Comma to Separate a Long or Compound Subject From Its Verb

If the subject is so long that it needs a marker
or boundary at the end, do not use the careless
device of an incorrect comma. Rewrite or re-
phrase the sentence. This fault is commonly
found in poorer legal prose.

Confusing: The dicta in recent Supreme Court
opinions and the explicit recognition of that Court's
authority by the lower courts, emphasize what was
first developed in *Brown v. Waters*.

Clear: (Omit the comma and rewrite) The dicta in
recent Supreme Court opinions emphasizes what was
first developed in *Brown v. Waters*. The lower
courts' explicit recognition of the Court's authority
has furthered that development.

(7) Use an Introductory Comma to Set Off Introductory Words, Phrases, or Clauses

If the introductory element is short and no misreading is possible, the comma may be omitted,
for example, "In 1975 the Corporation signed a

collective bargaining agreement with a union local."

Examples that invite misreading:

1. *Confusing omission of comma:* To summarize the question is difficult.

Clear: To summarize, the question is difficult. Or: The question is difficult to summarize.

2. *Confusing:* Contrary to the holding in *Bracton v. Blackstone* at that time the practice of submitting documentary evidence to a jury was long established.

Clear: Contrary to the holding in *Bracton v. Blackstone,* at that time the practice of submitting documentary evidence to a jury was long established.

(8) Use a Series Comma

Use a comma to mark each separate element in a series; that is, put a comma after each item and before the conjunction. (A, B, and C)

Confusing Omissions of Series Comma:

1. Both jobs require activities that are closely related, such as the teaching of sports skills, the supervision and coordination of practices and competitive activities. (Comma belongs after "practices.")

2. Although blood alcohol levels depend on various factors, including body weight, amount and type of food in the stomach and time between drinking and testing, the primary factor is the amount of alcohol ingested. (If no comma follows "stomach," the reader does not know where the series ends.)

3. The witnesses included one representative from Washington, Oregon, Montana and Nevada and Utah. (One from Montana and Nevada and another from Utah? Or one from Montana and another from Nevada and Utah?)

(9) Use a Contrasting Comma for Emphasis

Use a comma to emphasize contrast or to add emphasis to a particular word, phrase, or clause.

He sold non-existent property in Washington, not in Oregon.

(10) Use a Comma to Separate Dependent from Independent Clauses

If the dependent clause comes first, it should be separated from the independent clause by a comma. The comma may be omitted if the dependent clause follows the independent clause and is restrictive.

1. If an employee objects to a medical examination, the case must be considered individually.

2. A case must be considered individually if an employee objects to a medical examination.

(11) Do Not Use a Comma Before "Because"

Do not use a comma before "because" unless "because" introduces a nonrestrictive clause. That rarely happens.

Incorrect: This is contradictory to the common practice, because, according to the common practice, the title of ownership will not be transferred to the buyer until payment is completed.

Corrected: This is contradictory to the common practice because, according to the common practice, the title of ownership will not be transferred to the buyer until payment is completed.

(12) Use a Comma to Separate Some Adjectives

Coordinate adjectives are those that may be joined by "and": erratic, vague testimony ("erratic" and "vague" both modify "testimony").

Use no comma if the first adjective modifies the second adjective, that is, if "and" is not understood between them (thus, they are not coordinate):

"a good looking man"

"illegal drug traffic"

"grey striped cat" (if the stripes are grey, but "grey, striped cat" if the the cat is grey and striped)

(13) Use a Comma After Parenthetical Material

Use the comma after the parenthesis, not before.

Because the case was too old (1875), we omitted it.

(14) Place a Comma Inside Quotation Marks

Both a comma and a period are always placed inside quotation marks.

He is not classified as an "employee."

He is not an "employee," nor is he a union member.

(15) Use Commas With Numbers

Use a comma with dates, addresses, place names, statistics, measurements, and the like to increase readability.

January 18, 1980, (month and day, year,)

On January 18, 1,000 entries were received.

On 18 January 1980, we received your letter.

(c) Use of the Semicolon

(1) Use a Semicolon to Separate Two Sentences

Use a semicolon to separate two sentences:

(i) if joined without a connective:

It was 8:00 P.M.; the road was dry.

(ii) if joined with a conjunctive adverb, such as "however," "therefore," "moreover":

It was 8:00 P.M.; furthermore, the road was dry.

(iii) if joined with other transitional expressions, such as "in brief," "on the other hand":

It was 8:00 P.M.; contrary to testimony, the road was dry.

Do not use a semicolon if one sentence is incomplete (*i.e.*, a fragment), as in these examples:

1. Because lawyers are expected to think and speak well, they are expected to write well; when in fact many of them don't. (Use a comma since what follows the semicolon is a fragment.)

2. Mr. Gould replied that the NLRB would not discuss it; and would not need to. (Use no punctuation.)

(2) Use a Semicolon to Substitute for the Comma in a Complex Series

A semicolon should be substituted for a comma when internal punctuation obscures the main divisions of any series:

The witnesses we must locate are John Flanders, whose last address was Longmont, Colorado; W. F. Irmscher of Seattle, Washington; Robert E. Kelley, who moved to Juneau, Alaska; and Eleanor Laney of Dallas, Texas.

(3) Place a Semicolon Outside Quotation Marks

The witness replied, "I don't know"; however, the record shows that she did know.

When a direct quotation ends in a semicolon or colon, the semicolon or colon may be dropped.

(d) Use of the Colon

(1) Use a Colon to Introduce a List or an Enumeration

A colon may be used instead of a comma:

The plaintiff's legal position depends upon extracts from three decisions of the United States Supreme Court: *Anderson v. Shipowners, United Mine Workers v. Pennington,* and *Federal Maritime Commission v. Pacific Maritime Association.*

(2) Use a Colon to Indicate That Something Will Follow

What follows will usually be an example, illustration, or elaboration:

In *Anderson v. Shipowners,* the collective bargaining process was not used: a unilateral hiring procedure had already been set up by the Association.

(3) Use a Colon to Introduce Quotations or Formal Statements

The Court found that the activity was not permissible: "The shipowners have surrendered completely to the control of the Association, thus limiting the activities of both shipowners and seamen."

(4) Use a Colon to Emphasize What Follows

Not only is the report itself hearsay, but most of it is second- and third-level hearsay: the statements of numerous persons are summarized, quoted, or otherwise relied upon.

When a complete sentence follows a colon, the capital letter at the beginning of the sentence is optional.

Examples, both correct:

1. Lay readers can be helpful in several ways: (1) they have not been "desensitized" to the obfuscation and convolutions of legal writing, and (2) they can identify the words, sentences, or ideas that will be difficult for non-lawyers to understand.

2. Lay readers can be helpful in several ways: (1) They have not been "desensitized" to the obfuscation and convolutions of legal writing. (2) They can point out words, sentences, or ideas that will be difficult for non-lawyers to understand.

(5) Place a Colon Outside Quotation Marks

No one has denied Plaintiff's statement that "mortgage instruments should be comprehensible": the court agrees, the defendant agrees, and the general public agrees.

(e) Use of Parentheses

(1) Use Parentheses to Set Off Potentially Ambiguous Phrases

Sometimes parentheses are more reliable than commas for setting off phrases that are potentially ambiguous or that obscure the "main line" of the sentence.

Confusing: Borrowers must be informed of limits on transfer or sale of their property other than with the Bank's consent before they are asked to sign a loan instrument. (Does the bank consent *before* they sign?)

Clear: Borrowers must be informed of limits on transfer or sale of their property (other than with the Bank's consent) before they are asked to sign a loan instrument.

(2) Use Parentheses to Enclose Interruptions

Explanations, digressions, and other interruptions to the main thought of the sentence may be set off with parentheses.

The answer is "yes" and "no" (a lawyer-like response).

(3) Use Correct Punctuation With Parentheses

If the parentheses occur at the end of a sentence, the end punctuation goes outside the last parenthesis. If the parentheses contain a full sentence, punctuation goes inside the last parenthesis.

Law students must have writing exercises (as opposed to "search and destroy" missions in the library).

Law students must have writing exercises. (They should do more than "search and destroy missions" in the library.)

(4) Use Parentheses to Enclose Numbers and Letters Marking Divisions in the Main Text

A deed of trust must: (1) be comprehensible to lay readers, (2) accurately reflect the requirements of the lender, and (3) clearly inform lay borrowers of their obligations.

(f) Use of the Hyphen

Use a hyphen with a compound adjective when necessary to prevent ambiguity, as in "first-class," "well-written," "well-timed," "year-long," "decision-making," "job-related." As shown in the examples below, the problem is that one word may be read as the wrong part of speech.

1. *Confusing*: When the government financed research in the maritime industry declines . . . .. (Is the research government-financed, or does the government finance research?)

With hyphen: When the government-financed research in the maritime industry declines . . . ..

2. *Confusing*: Furthermore, the state sponsored schools throughout this area provide the greatest portion of NCAA funds. (Are the schools state-sponsored or does the state sponsor schools?)

With hyphen: Furthermore, the state-sponsored schools throughout this area provide the greatest portions of NCAA funds.

3. *Confusing*: Watch for heavy vehicle traffic. (Heavy vehicles or heavy traffic?)

With hyphen: Watch for heavy-vehicle traffic. (Watch for heavy vehicles.)

Use a hyphen to form compounds with numbers:

two-week trial

thirty-five-year-old defendant

five-year contract

(g) Use of a Dash

(1) Use the Dash Sparingly

The dash is the least defined mark of punctuation. It suggests a connection rather than describing it. The dash has connotations of stream-of-consciousness thought and carries a conversational tone.

The dash should be used sparingly in legal writing and then mainly to introduce a recapitulation. It may also be used strategically in an argument—for dramatic effect.

(2) Use a Dash to Indicate a Break, Shift, or Interruption

When law graduates begin to practice law—which for most lawyers means writing every day under pressure—they should already know how to write well.

(3) Use a Dash to Expand an Idea

Use of a dash to expand an idea is rhetorically effective when combined with repetition of a word or phrase.

As a result of this accident, Peter sustained severe and lasting injuries—so severe that his foot may require amputation.

(h) Use of the Slash or Virgule

The slash has become increasingly popular in legal writing and is nearly always misused. It should not be used to mean "and." It means "or." It indicates an "either-or" situation, that is, a choice of alternatives.

Do not use the slash for "and/or" if you mean both "and" and "or." It means one or the other, but not both. Do not use the slash for phrases like "public/private functions" if you mean both "public" and "private." It means "public" or "private," but not both.

Use a slash to indicate alternatives:

The car is available with a white/brown exterior and a black/beige interior.

The "will/shall" controversy is passé.

Use a slash to stand for "per" in abbreviations (40 mi./hr.).

(i) Use of Quotation Marks

Close quotation marks after a period or a comma. ("Quotation." "Quotation,") Close before semicolon or colon. ("Quotation"; "Quotation":)

Ordinarily, quotation marks are not required to enclose indented material unless indented material continues beyond one page. The indenting itself serves to punctuate the quotation. Note, however, that quotation marks are required for even indented quotations under some court rules.

Use a single quotation mark to indicate a quoted word or phrase within a quotation.

> As stated by the court, "Plaintiff's request for this relief is a 'red herring.' "

(j) Use of the Apostrophe

(1) Use an Apostrophe to Reflect Possession

Add apostrophe plus "s" or apostrophe alone.

woman's	everyone's
men's	Justices'

If a singular word ends in "s" and if an "'s" would make it hard to pronounce, simply add an apostrophe. The apostrophe is usually added if the syllable is pronounced as in "goodness's," but not in "for goodness' sake."

To show joint or individual possession in a series of nouns or pronouns, use the apostrophe in
the following manner:

Joint: "Williams, Green, and Mucklestone's policy" (the policy of the group or firm)

"James, Shannon, and Jane's property" (their joint
property)

Individual: "Williams' and Green's policies" (each
has a separate policy or policies)

"James's, Shannon's, and Jane's properties" (separate properties)

Do not use an apostrophe for possessives of
personal pronouns: his, hers, theirs, ours, yours,
its, whose.

(2) Use "Its" When You Need the
Possessive Form of "It"

Perhaps the most frequent of all writing errors
is the mistaken use of "its" for "it's" and vice
versa. "Its" is a possessive, meaning "belonging
to it." "It's" is the contraction of the two words
"it is." Although common, this error gives the
appearance of either sloppiness or ignorance.
The argument in the Opening Brief of Appellant
in an appeal case, for example, began with this
sentence:

There being no showing that the defendant exer-
cised dominion or control over the alcohol in his car,
it's mere presence in his unoccupied automobile, in
the face of unrebutted testimony that the beer was

[*218*]

owned solely by an adult, was insufficient to establish the defendant's constructive possession of the
alcohol beyond a reasonable doubt.

The mispunctuation of "its" in this convoluted
sentence may help to undermine the credibility of
the writer.

(3) Use an Apostrophe to Indicate Omission of Letters

it's (it is)

they're (they are)

who's (who is)

(4) Use an Apostrophe for Certain Plurals

Use an apostrophe to make the possessive of
plurals ending in "s."

First form the plural. If the plural ends in "s,"
add an apostrophe. If it does not, add " 's."

labor unions'	years'
lawyers'	Johnsons'
witnesses'	

Use " 's" to form plurals of words used as
words, of letters used as letters, and of numbers:

1. How many "yea's" are there?

2. The "7's" in the receipt are blurred.

3. "Occur" has two "c's" but only one "r."

[*219*]

(5) Use " 'S" With Gerunds But Not With Participles

Use " 's" with gerunds (verbs converted to nouns ending in "ing"). Use no " 's" with participles (verbs converted to adjectives ending in "ing"). Decide which one to use according to what you want to emphasize, the word ending in "ing" or the noun preceding it.

   1. The judge's leaving the court provoked comment. (Here, the gerund "leaving" is emphasized.)

   2. The judge leaving the court provoked comment. (Here, the judge is emphasized. "Leaving" is a participle modifying the noun "judge.")

   3. The court's holding in *Patner* set an important precedent. (emphasis on gerund "holding")

   4. The court holding in *Patner* set an important precedent. (emphasis on court)

(k) Use of the Exclamation Point

Unless an exclamation point occurs in a direct quotation, it should not be used by legal writers. It is rarely appropriate for professional writing of any kind.

Writers tend to use exclamation points to intensify or emphasize a point or idea. Rather than use an obvious, mechanical device, such as an exclamation point or underlining, select emphatic verbs and nouns.

(*1*) Use of Brackets

Brackets have the three following uses in legal writing. Use brackets to comment within a direct quotation:

> "Provision for a joint and survivor annuity is required beginning on the date the employer reaches the earliest retirement age [*i.e.*, age 50] or ten years prior to normal retirement age [*i.e.*, 65 minus 10 = 55]."

Do not use brackets casually, however, to tailor quotations to fit your sentences. Design your sentences to fit grammatically and thematically with the quoted material.

Use brackets to indicate change of lower to upper case or the reverse in the first letter of a direct quotation:

> 1. "[T]he site of the Company headquarters is the primary jurisdiction."

> 2. The booklet states that "[f]or a proper understanding of the Plan, the complete text should be read."

Use brackets to enclose a parenthetical expression inside parentheses:

> She fails to cite the only relevant section of ERISA (assuming that ERISA [section 205(b)] will govern).

(m) Punctuation of Citations

Citation sentences begin with capitals and end with periods. Citation clauses are set off from the rest of the text by a comma. Citations in a "string" are separated from one another by semicolons. (See the "Blue Book," *A Uniform System of Citation* for correct punctuation of introductory signals.)

(n) Punctuation of Structured Enumeration

Introduce an enumerated series with a colon. If the elements of the series are incomplete sentences, use no initial capitalization and punctuate with semicolons or commas or omit punctuation.

§ 8.3 GRAMMAR

(a) Subject-Verb Agreement

Verbs agree in number and person with the subject. The key to assuring agreement is to find the true subject and to determine whether it is singular or plural.

(1) Beware of Phrases Between Subject and Verb

Phrases coming between subject and verb do not affect the verb's form. Look for the true subject, especially where prepositional phrases come between subject and verb.

1. *One* of plaintiff's arguments *is* enough.

2. *Not one* of the witnesses *remembers* what happened.

3. *Principles of Medical Ethics*, published by the American Medical Association, *contains* provisions concerning confidential information.

(2) Beware of Lengthy Subject Phrases or Clauses

Agreement problems often occur where lengthy subject phrases or clauses separate subjects and verbs.

1. *Incorrect*: Washington's interest-analysis approach to choice of law problems *result* in the following holdings.

Corrected: Washington's interest-analysis *approach* to choice of law problems *results* in the following holdings.

2. *Incorrect*: The purpose for which a corporation may be organized under the title are "any lawful purpose or purposes, except for the purpose of banking."

Corrected: The *purpose* for which a corporation may be organized under the title *is* "any lawful purpose or purposes, except for the purpose of banking."

3. *Incorrect*: The correct use of quotation marks, enumeration, and a few other technical devices are briefly covered below.

Correct: The correct *use* of quotation marks, enumeration, and a few other technical devices *is* briefly covered below.

(3) Use a Plural Verb With Most Compound Subjects

1. *A plumber* and *a pipefitter make* more money than an English teacher.

2. *Cars* and *one truck were* trapped on the stranded ferry.

If the compound subject stands for a single unit, use a singular verb:

Finesse, Wrangle, and Pinch is a respectable firm.

If the compound subject consists of singular words joined by "or" or "nor," use a singular verb.

If *oral ridicule* or *a written statement* to a third person *causes* a person to be shunned or avoided, it may be defamatory.

Plural subjects joined by "or" or "nor" take plural verbs:

If neither written statements to a third party nor instances of oral ridicule *cause* a person to be shunned or avoided, then they are not defamatory.

If a singular subject and a plural subject are joined by "or" or "nor," make the verb agree with the nearer one:

If written statements to a third party or oral ridicule *causes* a person to be shunned or avoided, then there may be defamation.

(4) Use Singular Verbs With Most Indefinite Pronouns and Collective Nouns

Singular verbs may be used with the following pronouns and nouns:

all	every	nobody
another	everybody	someone
anything	everyone	something
each	everything	such a
each one	many a	
either	neither	

A few of these may be singular or plural depending on intended meaning: all, any, none, some, each, group, audience, committee, crowd.

In conversation, plural pronouns are frequently used to refer to singular nouns or pronouns, for example, "*Everyone* wants to have *their* efforts praised." This commonly occurs when people try to avoid using the singular pronouns "his" or "her." Nevertheless, in formal writing, subject-verb agreement should be precise and accurate.

Mass nouns take a singular verb unless they clearly have a plural meaning.

aesthetics	logistics	politics
economics	news	

(5) Make Forms of "to be" and Linking Verbs Agree With the Subject

A linking verb agrees with the subject, not the complement:

1. The *source* of the funds *is* the property sale and the liquid assets.

2. The *property sale* and the *liquid assets are* the source of the funds.

When forms of "to be" or verbs of being follow "there," they agree with the subject following:

1. There *are dozens* of unconvincing arguments.

2. There *is* no *reason* to try this case.

(b) Use of "Who" or "Whom"

Use the pronoun "who" when it will serve as a subject. Use the pronoun "whom" when it will serve as an object. In writing, the distinction should be carefully observed. In conversation, many people use "who" instead of "whom" because "whom" sounds unnatural or too formal. Most English speakers continue, however, to use "whom" in conversation whenever it follows a preposition—sometimes correctly, as in "You know of whom I speak" or "Give it to whom you like" or incorrectly, as in "The letter was lost by whomever received it."

In a few instances, determining the function of a relative pronoun may be difficult. Whether a relative pronoun serves as a subject or as an object is determined by its use in its own clause, not by whether its antecedent serves as a subject or as an object. For example, in "We know the ones who pay the bills," the relative pronoun's antecedent is "ones," which is the object of "know." Rather than using "whom," which serves as an object, the writer must use "who" because "who" is the subject of its own clause ("who pays the bills"). The entire clause "who pays the bills" stands in apposition to "ones."

1. We know *who* you are. (With this potentially confusing structure, "who" appears to serve both subject and object functions. However, if you ask *"what* do we know?" the answer becomes clear: We know "who you are." "Who you are" is a clause in which "who" is the subject-form following the linking verb "are." The object of the sentence is the entire unit "who you are.")

But: We know of *whom* you speak.

2. Checks were made of applicants *who* the landlord felt might not have been "congenial" tenants. ("Who" is the subject of the clause "who might not have been.")

But: Checks were made of applicants about *whom* the landlord had doubts.

3. Ask *who* the judge will be. (Here "who" is the subject-form following the verb "will be." The case must agree on either side of a linking verb, that is, subject and subject complement must be in the same case. Since "judge" is the subject, "who" must be used instead of "whom.")

But: *Whom* shall we ask to determine who the judge will be?

4. Mr. Tulkinghorn has been described as an oyster of the old school, *whom* nobody can open. ("Whom" is the object of the verb "can open.")

But: Mr. Tulkinghorn, *who* has been described as an oyster of the old school, cannot be opened.

(c) Use of Personal Pronouns

Whenever the first person pronoun replaces the subject, it must be "I." Whenever the first person pronoun replaces the object, it must be "me." Errors commonly occur when two or more pronouns are used together or when normal sentence order is inverted.

1. *Incorrect*: The trial was scheduled at the convenience of Ms. Kroenke, Mrs. Katz, Mr. Wimsy, and *I*.

Correct: The trial was scheduled at the convenience of Ms. Kroenke, Mrs. Katz, Mr. Wimsy, and *me*.

2. *Correct*: He thought the witness was *I*. (*Not*: "was me")

3. *Correct*: It is *I*. (In conversation, the usage "It's me" is entirely established and acceptable. In writing, however, the correct form should be used.)

4. *Correct*: The court can read the record as well as *we*. (To decide, simply fill in the missing words "as well as we can.")

Whenever the third person singular pronoun replaces the subject, it must be "he" or "she."

Whenever the third person singular pronoun replaces the object, it must be "him" or "her."

1. This is she. ("She" is the subject complement and must make sense on either side of "is," thus "she is she," not "her is she.")

2. It was *he* who argued. (*Not*: It was *him* who argued.)

3. It was *they* who requested the postponement. (*Not*: It was them who requested the postponement.)

4. Mr. Gann thought her to be *me*. (To test this, reverse "me" and "her." "Thought me to be her," not "thought I to be her.")

(d) Use of Reflexive Pronouns

The reflexive pronouns are myself, yourself, ourselves, herself, himself, and themselves. Reflexive pronouns have two uses: to reflect back on an agent (The *witness* perjured *himself*) and to emphasize something already named (*I myself* wrote the brief).

Do not use reflexive pronouns instead of personal pronouns.

1. *Incorrect*: Ms. Street and myself took the depositions.

Correct: *Ms. Street and I* took the depositions.

2. *Incorrect*: The document was signed by Mr. Throgmorton and myself.

Correct: The document was signed by *Mr. Throgmorton and me.*

(e) Which to Use: "Who," "Which," or "That"

"Who" or "whom" is used to refer to a person.

She is the lawyer *whom* I mentioned.

He is the one *who* ran for office.

"Which" is used to refer to everything except a person.

The evidence, *which* he misplaced, would have resolved the case.

We had never seen golden pheasants, *which* are more brilliantly plumed than parrots.

"That" is used to refer to either persons or things.

She is the representative *that* I mentioned.

We had never seen the golden pheasants *that* Mr. Clark raised.

(f) Pronoun Reference

(1) Avoid Pronoun Confusion by Using Proper Names or by Repeating the Antecedent

Meaning is more important here than "elegant variation."

Confusing: The *servant's* liability stems from the duty owed to a *third person* under the law to conduct *himself* so as not to injure others.

Clear: The servant's liability stems from the duty owed to a third person under the law requiring the servant to act so as not to injure others.

(2) Avoid the Indefinite Use of "It"

The use of "it" in legal writing causes more confusion than any other pronoun reference. Avoid "it" whenever possible.

Confusing: In this case, it is sought to carry forward, as it were, an anterior negligent omission of the defendants, though continuing, it is true, up to the time of the occurrence, and to assign to it the whole blame for the occurrence although by no effort of the defendants or of their servants could it at that stage have been prevented.

Clearer: In this case, plaintiff seeks to carry forward an anterior negligent omission of the defendants that continued up to the time of the injury and to assign to the omission the whole blame for the injury, although by no effort of the defendants or of their servants could the injury at that stage have been prevented.

Avoid phrases like "found it advisable." As Lewis Carroll demonstrates in *Alice in Wonderland*, this can be confusing:

"The patriotic archbishop of Canterbury found it advisable—"

"Found what?" said the Duck.

"Found *it*," the Mouse replied rather crossly: "Of course you know what 'it' means."

"I know what 'it' means well enough, when *I* find a thing," said the Duck: "It's generally a frog, or a worm. The question is, what did the archbishop find?"

(g) Use of Sex-Linked Pronouns

Many readers object to the use of masculine pronouns to indicate both sexes. Writers, on the other hand, have difficulty replacing them. When you face this problem, first try to avoid using any pronoun. If this approach will not work in a particular situation, try to change a singular pronoun to a plural.

1. *With pronoun*: A taxpayer may obtain a refund from the IRS by amending her returns for 1976, 1977, and 1978.

Without pronoun: A taxpayer may obtain a refund from the IRS by amending returns for 1976, 1977, and 1978.

With plural pronoun: Taxpayers may obtain a refund from the IRS by amending their returns for 1976, 1977, and 1978.

2. *With pronouns*: A witness may be able to complain of nuisance even though the plant has a dust easement on his or her property.

With plural pronoun: Witnesses may be able to complain of nuisance even though the plant has a dust easement on their property.

If a singular pronoun must be used, the "he or she" form is preferable to either "he" or "she" alone. Although using "he or she," "his or hers," and "him or her" adds extra words and may be clumsy, it is usually accurate.

On printed forms, the use of "she/he" and "his/her" allows the individual user to cross out the inappropriate choice. The odd-looking "s/he" may save time in writing informal memoranda, but it should not appear in formal legal writing.

The third-person pronoun "one" may also be used to avoid the "he or she" problem. The pronoun "one," however, carries a formal tone, sometimes even a pompous tone, as in "One can hardly imagine oneself making such an argument." A few rare phrases are improved by replacing "man" with "one." The sentence "No man should trespass on another man's property" becomes "No one should trespass on another's property." Few opportunities of this kind, other than in statute drafting, are available to legal writers. Regardless of the solution found to the sex-linked pronoun dilemma, wording should be consistent within the same piece of work.

(h) Use of Subjunctive Mood

Although the subjunctive mood is disappearing from English, it still may be used to indicate a supposed, imagined, contingent, or nonfactual action or state.

If her lawyer had succeeded, they would not now be bankrupt.

If settlement were possible, I would agree to it.

Whether the case be won or lost, we will get our fee.

Compare these forms of indicative and subjunctive:

Indicative	*Subjunctive*
I am; you are	If I be; If you be
I was; he was	If I were; If he were
I will be	If I should be
I will have been	If I should have been

§ 8.4　MECHANICS

Mechanics appropriate for legal writing may differ from those customarily used in other fields. The mechanics recommended here accord with the "Blue Book," *A Uniform System of Citation* (13th ed., 1981). See the "Blue Book" for further discussion of required form.

(a) Use of Italics

Underlining is used in typewritten or handwritten work to show italics.

Use italics for foreign words and phrases unless they have been anglicized (*joie de vivre*, but tortilla).

Use italics for the following Latin words and phrases, when used in legal writing. (Most other Latin words and phrases commonly used in legal writing are presumed to have been incorporated into the language of the law, thus are not underlined.)

qua	*quaere*
infra	*semble*

*inter alia
 (alios)*
inter se (sese)   *sub nom.*
passim   *supra*

Use italics for signals used to introduce citations of authority:

E.g.,   *But see*
Accord   *But cf.*
See   *See generally*
Cf.   *See also*
Compare . . .   *Contra*
   with . . .

"See" is not underlined if it is part of an introductory textual phrase, however, as in, "For a discussion of the tortious interference rule, see *Restatement (Second) of Torts* § 766A and comments (1978)."

Use italics for names of cases, books, periodical articles, newspapers, ships, and aircraft (when used in text; the rule for use in footnotes may differ):

Spectre v. Bond, 107 F. Supp. 70 (D.Mass.1972)

New York Times

Princess Marguerite

Air Force One

Use italics sparingly for words or phrases the writer wishes to emphasize. Italics or underlining for emphasis must not be used routinely, or all effect will be lost.

1. We are not concerned with *opinions* but with *facts*.

2. Washington's strong public policy against punitive damages should *not* be subordinated to other state policies.

The most common use of underlining for emphasis is inside quotations, for example:

Payment does not begin until Retirement Date; that date is the *later of* (1) date of entitlement or (2) month following 6-month absence for medical reasons. (emphasis added)

(b) Use of Ellipsis Points

Three points signal omission of a word or words in a quotation.

"Give me liberty or . . . death."

Do not begin a quotation with ellipsis points. Rather, use one of the following alternatives.

1. The Court held that the defendant "did not satisfy the conditions of the contract."

2. "[L]egal writers have a difficult audience: overworked judges."

Indicate omission of language from the end of a sentence by an ellipsis between the last word quoted and the final punctuation. In the following example, the fourth point is the sentence period.

> *Full sentence*: "A board of directors selected by vote of the shareholders shall have the authority to discharge for sufficient cause all certificated and uncertificated employees according to the bylaws of the corporation."

> *With Ellipsis*: A board of directors "shall . . . discharge for sufficient cause all certificated and uncertificated employees . . . ."

If a fully quoted sentence is followed by ellipsis, four periods are used. The first period is simply the normal sentence period. The remaining three periods are the usual ellipsis points.

> "Readability is always lessened by long sentences. . . . [L]ong paragraphs also tire the reader."

> (Ellipsis here means that words at the beginning of the second sentence have been omitted. If the capital "L" were not bracketed, omission of a full sentence would be indicated.)

If one or more entire paragraphs are omitted, use four points and indent them. Then begin the next paragraph on the next line. If the first word in a second or subsequent paragraph is omitted, show the omission by indenting three points. (If a quotation begins in mid-paragraph, simply begin at the indented margin without ellipsis.)

When typing, leave a space before the first ellipsis point and after the last. If an ellipsis follows a complete sentence, however, then the sentence period is placed immediately after the last letter of the last word in the sentence. For example, "Readability is always lessened by long sentences. . . ."

(c) Use of Numerals

In text, spell out the numbers zero to ninety-nine. In footnotes, spell out the numbers zero to nine. Use numerals for numbers over ninety-nine in text and for numbers over nine in footnotes.

Always spell out a number that begins a sentence.

Spell out round numbers like "thousand," "million," "hundred," if you wish. Simply be consistent.

If numbers over and under 100 occur in a series, use numerals for all. Items in a series containing only numbers under 100 should be spelled out.

Numerals should be used consistently for section numbers or other subdivision numbers, for percentages or dollar amounts, and for numbers containing a decimal point.

(d) Typographical Conventions

Leave no space before, after, or between the two hyphens that make up a dash.

Leave one space between the section symbol (§) and the numeral: 28 U.S.C. § 2482.

Leave no space between the dollar sign and the numerals ($5.00) and the percentage sign and the numerals (7%).

If a symbol begins a sentence, write the word for the symbol out in full, for example, "Section 2482 was added in 1972." Do not begin a sentence with a symbol.

SELECTED REFERENCES

GENERAL LEGAL WRITING

N. Brand & J. White, *Legal Writing: The Strategy of Persuasion* (1976).

An excellent introduction to writing for law students, with exercises and samples for examination writing.

H. Weihofen, *Legal Writing Style* (2d ed. 1980).

The classic book on writing about legal matters.

R. Wydick, *Plain English for Lawyers* (1979).

A slim volume covering some basics with excellent exercises and answers.

GENERAL COMPOSITION AND GRAMMAR

J. Opdycke, *Harper's English Grammar* (1965).

The most comprehensive and reliable guide to grammar available to the non-specialist. Available in paperback.

W. Irmscher, *The Holt Guide to English* (3d ed. 1981).

One of the most popular undergraduate handbooks incorporating advice on grammar, punctuation, mechanics, and style in a clear and usable way. Neither idiosyncratic nor experimental; useful for writers at any level.

Pence and Emery, *A Grammar of Present-Day English* (2d ed. 1963).

A grammarian's grammar, containing thorough treatment of diagramming, which lawyers and judges may find useful. With exercises.

Strunk and White, *The Elements of Style* (3d ed. 1979).

Brief (85 pages), widely-used paperback guide to general writing. Useful as an introduction to popular discourse; parts of the style section not helpful for legal writing.

LANGUAGE

T. Bernstein, *The Careful Writer* (1965).

A modern usage manual that is readily available in paperback.

W. Burton, *Legal Thesaurus* (Reg. ed. 1981).

A useful source of inspiration for synonyms and associated legal concepts for more than 5,000 words in legal contexts.

B. & C. Evans, *A Dictionary of Contemporary American Usage* (1965).

W. Follett, *Modern American Usage* (Barzun ed. 1966).

Fowler's Modern English Usage (2d ed., E. Gowers 1965).

Now somewhat dated, but still recommended for law review writers by the editors of the

13th edition of the "Blue Book." See Citations and Mechanics, *infra.* For a contemporary conservative equivalent, see W. & M. Morris, *Harper Dictionary of Contemporary Usage* (1975), written in conjunction with a panel of 136 distinguished consultants on usage.

D. Mellinkoff, *The Language of the Law* (1963).

A fine historical approach to legal language, written by a lawyer. Entertaining and instructive.

Webster's New International Dictionary (2d ed. 1930).

Now more than 50 years old, but regarded by many as the most comprehensive and authoritative dictionary. Still preferred by many over the Third Edition Merriam-Webster New International Dictionary.

OFFICE RESEARCH MEMORANDA

E. Re, *Brief Writing and Oral Argument* (4th ed. 1974).

M. Rombauer, *Legal Problem Solving: Analysis, Research and Writing* (3d ed. 1978).

APPELLATE BRIEFS

R. Stern, *Appellate Practice in the United States* (1981).

The chapter on "Brief Writing" covers details not discussed elsewhere. Describes and discusses different forms and contents required for briefs by the differing state court rules.

F. Wiener, *Briefing and Arguing Federal Appeals* (1967).

UCLA Moot Court Honors Program Handbook of Appellate Advocacy (rev. ed. 1980).

A manual that is useful for student moot court work.

See also the Re and Rombauer books, *supra*, under "Office Research Memoranda," and Weihofen under "General Legal Writing."

CITATIONS AND MECHANICS

A Uniform System of Citation (13th ed. 1981).

Published and distributed by the Harvard Law Review Association, this "Blue Book" is the final guide on structure, content, and form of legal citations and on some rules of mechanics (abbreviations, numerals, symbols, italicization, capitalization, and court titles).

LAW SCHOOL EXAMINATIONS

S. Kinyon, *Introduction to Law Study and Law Examinations in a Nutshell* (1971).

Contains discussion and examples of examination answers. The focus is more on the thinking process than on the writing process. For greater focus on the writing process, see the Brand & White book, *supra*, under "General Legal Writing."

SELECTED REFERENCES

RHETORIC

B. Christensen, *Notes Toward a New Rhetoric* (2d ed. 1978).

Contains essays about research in composition and psycholinguistics as these apply to professional writing.

E. Corbett, *Classical Rhetoric for the Modern Student* (2d ed. 1971).

A compilation of the classical techniques for persuasion and argument. Much of it is directly applicable to argumentative legal writing. Contains a section on judicial discourse.

E. Hirsch, *The Philosophy of Composition* (1977).

Well received historical and contemporary review of scholarship in composition. Recommended for teachers of writing.

RECENT PUBLICATIONS

The following are recently published books about legal writing and drafting. They became available too late for our careful review before completion of the *Nutshell* manuscript. Each appears, however, to offer useful suggestions from differing viewpoints.

G. Block, *Effective Legal Writing* (1981).

R. Dickerson, *Materials on Legal Drafting* (1981).

SELECTED REFERENCES

J. Dernbach & R. Singleton II, *A Practical Guide to Legal Writing and Legal Method* (1981).

C. Felsenfeld & A. Siegel, *Writing Contracts in Plain English* (1981).

G. Gopen, *Writing from a Legal Perspective* (1981).

D. Mellinkoff, *Legal Writing: Sense and Nonsense* (1981).

*

INDEX

Italics indicates references to explanations of word usages. References are to Pages.

INDEX

References are to Pages

INDEX

References are to Pages

INDEX

References are to Pages

INDEX

References are to Pages

INDEX

References are to Pages

INDEX

References are to Pages

INDEX

References are to Pages

INDEX

References are to Pages

INDEX

References are to Pages

[*258*]

INDEX

References are to Pages

[*259*]

INDEX

INDEX

References are to Pages

[*261*]

INDEX

References are to Pages

INDEX

References are to Pages

INDEX

INDEX

References are to Pages

INDEX

References are to Pages

INDEX
References are to Pages

INDEX

INDEX

References are to Pages

INDEX

References are to Pages

INDEX

References are to Pages

[*271*]

INDEX

References are to Pages

INDEX

References are to Pages

INDEX

References are to Pages

[*277*]

INDEX
References are to Pages

INDEX

References are to Pages

INDEX

INDEX

References are to Pages

INDEX

References are to Pages

INDEX

References are to Pages

INDEX
References are to Pages

INDEX

References are to Pages

INDEX

References are to Pages

INDEX

References are to Pages

†